AMERICANS INTO ORBIT
The Story of Project Mercury

Here is a revised, up-to-date edition of a book which has proved unusually popular with young readers.

With great clarity, Gene Gurney describes the complex activities of Project Mercury—the designing, constructing and testing of the space capsule, the establishing of the Cape Canaveral Control Center and tracking stations, the selection and training of the seven astronauts, and the exciting flights of the first courageous space pilots.

Gene Gurney is a lieutenant colonel in the U.S. Air Force. He covers the next exciting stage of the United States manned space program in another Landmark Book, *Walk in Space: The Story of Project Gemini.*

AMERICANS INTO ORBIT

The Story of Project Mercury

Gene Gurney

Illustrated with photographs   Random House N.Y.

Third revised edition

PHOTOGRAPH CREDITS. The pictures used in this book are from the National Aeronautics and Space Administration, with the following exceptions: Bettmann Archive—page 35; British Information Service—page 29 (left); Esther C. Goddard—page 37 (right); Sovfoto—page 136; U.S. Air Force—page 29 (right); U.S. Army—pages 45, 53; U.S. Navy—page 51 (left); Wide World—pages 41, 51 (right), 59, 65 (top), 69 (bottom), 77, 143 (bottom), 147 (bottom), 149, 155 (top), 161 (top), 166

CONTENTS

AMERICANS INTO ORBIT
The Story of Project Mercury

I. PROJECT MERCURY SENDS A MAN INTO SPACE

Cape Kennedy is a wedge-shaped strip of sand jutting
out into the Atlantic from Florida's east coast. Until
1963, when it was renamed in honor of President John F.
Kennedy, it was called Cape Canaveral. At one time the
area was almost unknown, except to local residents, but
on the morning of May 5, 1961, it seemed that there
could be no one in the United States who hadn't heard
of Cape Canaveral. Everybody was talking about what
was happening there. People listened to transistor radios
as they walked along the street. They gathered in groups
to discuss the latest news bulletins.

"There has been a delay down at the Cape," they
said. Then: "They're counting again! Things are moving along now!"

What was happening at Cape Canaveral on that fine,
spring morning?

No longer a lonely stretch of sandy beach, Cape
Canaveral was now part of the Atlantic Missile Range—
the place from which the United States hoped to send
a man on a ride through space. After months of planning and preparation everything was at last ready for

the momentous journey. Since long before dawn the
Cape had been bright with lights as tense workers got
ready to send the first American into space.

Who was he? Who was this brave man who was
going to travel to a point more than 100 miles above
the surface of the earth? His name was Alan B. Shepard, Jr., and he was one of the seven astronauts of
Project Mercury.

Project Mercury was the name given to the United
States' program for putting a space capsule with a man
in it into orbit around the earth. During the flight,
scientists would study man's ability to survive in space.
Then, perhaps most important of all, the man and the
capsule were to be returned safely to earth.

Before a capsule with a human passenger could be
sent into orbit, it was first necessary to send one just
part of the way to be sure that everything was working
as it should. And that was what was happening at
Cape Canaveral on the morning of May 5. A manned
Mercury capsule was going to be shot more than 100
miles up into space, above the earth's atmosphere. Then
it would come back down again.

It was an important test. If the flight was a success,
Project Mercury would be well on the way to sending a
man all the way around the earth. Failure would mean
many months of work before the test could be tried
again.

There was a special reason why the attention of the
whole country was centered on Cape Canaveral. The
Soviet Union had already sent a man into space. They

Aerial view showing the construction of guided missile launching pads at Cape Canaveral, Florida.

had done it three weeks earlier, on April 12. Their spaceship, named the *Vostok,* which means "East," had gone completely around the earth in 87 minutes. It had carried a young man named Yuri Gagarin, the world's first spaceman.

The Soviet Union's announcement had been a great shock to the American people, who had always considered themselves to be leaders in science. It meant that the Soviet Union had taken the lead in the important business of sending a man into space.

The first American space flight had been scheduled for Tuesday, May 2. The weather forecast had not been good, and the day proved to be too cloudy for cameras to record the flight properly. Two days passed before the next try.

On Friday the weather was better. Astronaut Alan Shepard's big day began shortly after one o'clock in the morning when he was awakened in his room in Cape Canaveral's Hangar S. Sharing the room with him was John Glenn, the astronaut who had been chosen to take Shepard's place in case Shepard was unable to make the trip. In all, there were seven astronauts in the Project Mercury program. Three of them had been chosen as possibilities for the first Mercury flight, and Shepard had been picked as the one to go. John Glenn was his alternate. The third astronaut, Virgil Grissom, was on hand to help.

Both Alan Shepard and John Glenn had been getting ready for the trip into space. Since Saturday they had been on a special low-residue diet. They had taken, and passed, numerous physical checkups. Their home had been Hangar S. Now they went to eat the special breakfast that had been prepared for them — orange juice, eggs, steak, and toast. America's first spaceman was not going to be hungry during his trip.

There was one last physical examination for both men. Shepard proved to be in excellent shape for the flight. He would be the one to go.

The astronaut began the complicated process of getting dressed for a trip into space. First he put on long underwear which was patched in several places with a screenlike material through which air could circulate freely. On his feet were white socks and a pair of canvas slippers. Then doctors attached instruments called sensors to various places on his body. The sensors would tell them how the astronaut reacted to his flight through space. The scientists wanted to find out what happened to his temperature. Would it go up or down? Would his heart beat rapidly when he was hurtling along at 5,180 miles an hour? Would he have trouble breathing? This information was important to the future of America's space program.

The astronaut had to be helped into his space suit. It was a one-piece suit, made of nylon and rubber, which tied at his chest, legs, and arms. The outside was coated with a silvery, aluminum-like substance that would protect the astronaut from heat and radiation.

The Project Mercury pressure suit had been selected after six months of testing three possible choices. The suits were worn for as long as 24 hours at a time to

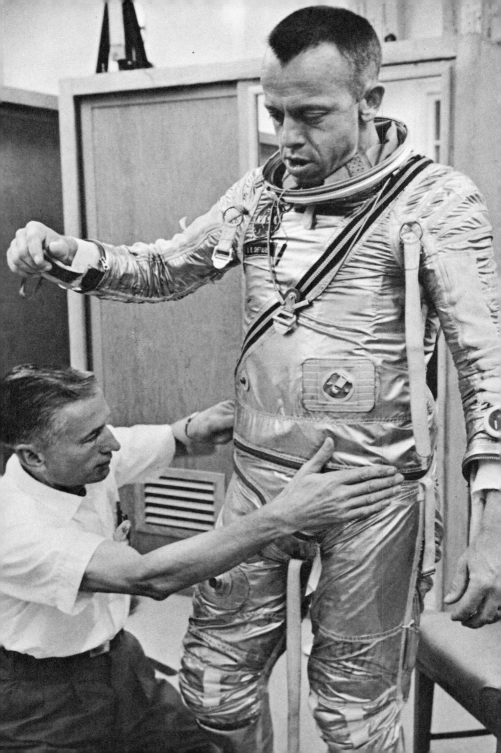

find out how comfortable they were. They were tried out in temperatures as high as 180 degrees. The one that was finally chosen was a modification of a pressurized flight suit that had been developed by the Navy. The National Aeronautics and Space Administration ordered 20 of them from the B. F. Goodrich Company. They cost about $4,000 each. The astronauts were supplied with two custom-fitted suits apiece.

Air flows into the suit at the waist and circulates through the underwear-like suit beneath it. The air is then exhausted through a pipe in the helmet and sent to an air-conditioning system located beneath the astronaut's couch. After purification it is recirculated through the pressure suit.

The suit would be inflated only if the cabin pressurization system failed. Then it would automatically supply the pressure needed to keep the astronaut alive in space. Under ordinary conditions the suit serves as an air-conditioning system in addition to the one built into the capsule. It helps keep the astronaut comfortable.

For Shepard's feet there were silver-colored boots. On his head he wore a helmet that looked very much like the kind football players wear, but it contained radio microphones and earphones and it had a plastic facepiece. The helmet was secured to a metal ring at the neck of the space suit. For his hands there were gloves which fastened to his sleeves.

After the pressurization of his suit had been checked, the astronaut was ready to go. Outside Hangar S a van was waiting to take him to his space capsule.

On the morning of the fateful day Astronaut Alan Shepard gets into his space suit in Hangar S.

At Pad 5, the launching site, missile crews and Project Mercury officials had been on the job for hours. There were a great many things to be done before a man could be sent into space.

It was shortly after five o'clock and still dark when Shepard left the van at Pad 5. There, high above him, was the capsule in which he would ride. Beneath it was the Redstone rocket that would boost it up into space. The Redstone rocket had been chosen for the first space flight because it was the most reliable of all America's rockets. Long and slender, its sides were covered with frost from the liquid oxygen that was escaping in great clouds. Liquid oxygen, or lox, in combination with ethyl alcohol, would provide the fuel for the rocket's engine.

The astronaut, in his silver suit, paused for one last look around him. Huge floodlights gave an almost unreal sharpness to the scene. The capsule, which had been named Freedom 7 by Shepard, was still covered by a green plastic work platform. An elevator would carry Shepard up the 60 feet to this "greenhouse."

As he got into the elevator, a cheer arose from the launching-pad crewmen. There were cries of "Good luck!" and "Have a good trip!" These men and hundreds more had worked hard to make this Project Mercury flight a success.

John Glenn was waiting on the platform outside Freedom 7. He had given the ten-by-six-foot capsule a thorough preflight check. Everything was ready to go.

Shepard talked briefly with Glenn and with Virgil

Shepard is helped onto the gantry elevator, which will take him up to his capsule.

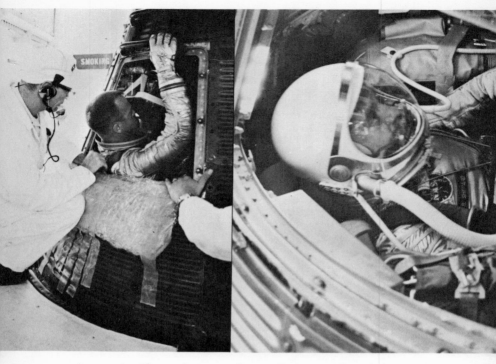

Astronaut Shepard enters his space craft, Freedom 7, from which he communicates during countdown with flight controllers in the Cape Canaveral blockhouse.

Grissom, who had joined them on the platform. At 5:20 A.M. he climbed into the capsule. White-gowned technicians helped him through the narrow hatch.

Attached to the instrument panel, where no one but Alan Shepard could see it, John Glenn had left a note. It said, No HANDBALL PLAYING IN THIS AREA. This made the astronaut laugh, because there was barely room enough for one man inside the tiny cockpit. John Glenn laughed too and then removed his sign.

The skillful hands of the technicians fastened the straps that held Shepard to his contour couch, made the final connections into his pressure suit, and took care of the necessary last-minute adjustments.

Then Guenter Wendt, pad leader for the launching, reached in for a final handshake and a last "Good luck!" The hatch door was pushed into place and fastened. The time was 6:10.

Alan Shepard got busy at once. He had many things to do—check lists to run through, switches to test, instruments to watch. And he was in telephone contact with the blockhouse, where technicians and Project Mercury officials were keeping an electronic watch on the Redstone, the capsule, and the astronaut.

All this time the rocket and the capsule had been surrounded by a red-and-white service tower called a gantry. Shortly after 6:30, just as the sun was rising, the workers finished the things that had to be done outside the capsule. The gantry, which was on tracks, was rolled away. Now everyone could see the gray-black Mercury capsule, shaped something like a television tube, standing high in the air above the slender Redstone rocket. Above the capsule a bright-orange escape rocket on a 16-foot tripod caught the sun's first rays. If something went wrong immediately after the launching, the escape rocket would carry the capsule and its passenger safely away from the Redstone.

A countdown precedes every rocket launching at Cape Canaveral. In a countdown the letter "T" stands for take-off time. T minus 20 means that there are still 20 minutes to go. At T zero the rocket is fired. When something goes wrong and has to be fixed, the countdown stops. The delay is known as a hold.

The countdown for the Mercury launching had reached T minus 15 when clouds rolled in over the Cape. Scientists expected to learn a great deal from pictures taken of the launching and the first few seconds of the rocket's flight. So the count became "T minus 15 and holding," while a recheck was made on the weather.

Then it was discovered that an inverter, a device for changing direct current to alternating current, wasn't working properly. The gantry had to be rolled back into position around the rocket to enable technicians to locate the trouble.

Eighty-six minutes later the inverter was fixed, and the gantry was rolled away. The weather had improved, so the countdown was resumed.

Then there was another hold. By this time Astronaut Shepard had been in the capsule for almost four hours, lying strapped to his contour couch. But this latest hold was just a short one—to check a pressure gauge.

"T minus 2!"

Time for a last communication from the blockhouse. Time to set the temperature controls for the pressure suit and the capsule cabin. The periscope through which Shepard had been able to watch what was happening on the ground was retracted into the capsule.

The count was in seconds now: "10, 9, 8, 7, 6, 5, 4, 3, 2, 1, firing command!"

"Ignition . . . Mainstage . . . Lift-off!"

From the capsule came the answer, "Roger, lift-off, and the clock is started."

Exactly at lift-off the astronaut had started a stop watch. With a roar the Redstone was on its way, lifting Freedom 7 and its passenger up, up, up.

Within the capsule America's first spaceman had braced himself for the rapid climb into space. His instruments told him what was happening. Through his headphones he could hear the Capsule Communicator who was monitoring his flight at the Mercury Control Center. From his capsule he could transmit messages to the Control Center to let them know how things were going.

The first minute of flight, as the rocket started its climb, was smooth—smoother than the astronaut had expected. Then the capsule began to vibrate as it reached supersonic speed and passed through the zone where its speed met the greatest resistance from the air. This didn't last long, however.

Soon Shepard was able to report: "O.K. It's a lot smoother now. A lot smoother."

Two minutes after take-off the Redstone rocket had

carried the Mercury capsule to a height of 25 miles. Shepard could feel the acceleration pushing him back into his couch. His heart was pumping hard, and all the air seemed to have been squeezed out of his lungs.

Right on schedule, after a little more than two minutes of flight, the Redstone's engine burned out. Now Shepard could feel his forward speed decrease.

But things began to happen fast. With a roaring noise, the escape tower, no longer needed, blew off. Then it was time for the capsule to leave the burned-out rocket. This was the most critical moment of the flight. If the rocket and the capsule didn't separate, Shepard would try to bail out. In all probability rocket, capsule, and astronaut would fall back into the ocean.

However, the explosive bolts in the clamp holding the capsule to the rocket fired as they were supposed to. The clamp fell away, and three small rockets in the capsule lifted it away from the spent Redstone.

With relief the astronaut heard the three rockets go off. When he saw the green light on his instrument panel, he reported: "Cap. sep. is green."

The capsule had now reached a point where the force of its motion away from the earth was exactly equal to the force of gravity pulling it toward the earth. Freedom 7 and its passenger were both weightless. Shepard was strapped to his couch, but he could feel the absence of all pressure. He reported it pleasant and relaxing. He was able to breathe, move, and talk without difficulty. He observed that the ends of his straps seemed to be floating in the air.

The slender gray-black Mercury-Redstone III soars into the air, carrying the first American into space.

The capsule had been in a slow 180-degree turn which placed its blunt end forward. That end contained a heat-dispersing shield to protect the capsule from the great heat it would encounter on reëntering the earth's atmosphere. The turn-about was completed, and the periscope had come back out. The busy astronaut had no time to look at the view. He was about to fly the capsule himself.

So far, Freedom 7 had been on automatic pilot, flying a controlled, pre-set course. Now Shepard took over. He raised and lowered the blunt end, turned the capsule from side to side, and finally took over control of the roll motion. He was flying his space ship!

Then he looked out through the periscope. He was a hundred miles above the earth. "What a beautiful view!" he exclaimed.

He could see northward as far as the Carolina coast, all the way west across Florida to Tampa Bay. To the south he could make out some of the islands in the Bahamas. The ocean was a deep, deep blue shading off to light green where the water was shallow. The sky was deep blue, too, almost black, because at that height there were no dust particles to reflect light.

All this time Freedom 7 had been climbing. The Redstone rocket could not lift the capsule high enough to send it into orbit. It was making a suborbital, or ballistic, flight, following a high, curving arc. When its forward motion was spent it would fall back to earth. A space ship actually in orbit, however, would continue on its path around the earth for a long time. It would be traveling so high and so fast that its forward motion would counteract the force of gravity pulling it toward the earth. To get such a spaceship out of orbit, it would first be necessary to slow down the capsule. The slowing down would also reduce the force with which the spaceship hit the earth's atmosphere as it came down.

This first attempt was a practice flight for that first trip into orbit around the earth. Although Freedom 7 could get down without it, Astronaut Shepard got ready for the firing of three braking rockets attached to the capsule's blunt end. They were called retro-rockets and would be needed when Project Mercury sent a man into orbit. He raised the blunt end of the capsule. The rockets fired in sequence.

"Retro 1 fired, very smooth," he reported.

Then: "Retro 2. Retro 3. All three retros are fired."

Freedom 7, which had reached a height of 116.5 miles above the earth, slowed and then started down.

The used rockets were supposed to be jettisoned automatically. Through his periscope Shepard could see the straps that held the rockets fall. But his instrument panel did not show the green light that meant the rockets were safely out of the way.

He told the Control Center: "I do not have a light. I see the straps falling away. I heard a noise. I will use override."

He then pushed the override button, which had been installed to take care of just such a failure in the automatic system.

His next transmission to the Control Center was: "Override used. The light is green."

Shepard had now pointed his capsule down at a 40-degree angle. Once again the capsule encountered increasing resistance. As Freedom 7 penetrated the earth's atmosphere, the 160-pound Shepard was feeling a pressure of 1,760 pounds. He managed to grunt out, "O.K., O.K., O.K.," to tell the men at the Control Center that the pressure wasn't too much for him.

The temperature in the capsule remained a comfortable 85 degrees as the spaceship rushed through the rapidly thickening atmosphere.

So far everything had gone without a hitch. But the astronaut still had ahead of him a landing in the ocean. The Mercury Control Center had been keeping a careful watch on the capsule's flight. The scientists there could tell that Freedom 7 was going to land just where they expected. "Your impact will be right on the button," they told the astronaut.

That was good news, for it meant that he would land where ships and planes were waiting to snatch him quickly from the water.

When the descending capsule reached 21,000 feet, a small parachute called a drogue was released from its narrow end. It helped to slow the capsule and keep it steady. At 10,000 feet the main parachute, a huge orange-and-white canopy, came out. It would lower the capsule into the water as gently as possible.

To get ready for the water landing, Shepard opened the face plate of his helmet and removed some of the

A Marine helicopter hooks onto Freedom 7 and Astronaut Shepard, in body harness, is pulled to safety.

straps that had been holding him to his couch.
Through a porthole he could see the water racing up
to meet him. He was getting close. He braced himself
and—*smack!*—he had landed.

The capsule went down into the water and over on
its side. Then it slowly righted itself. As soon as his
radio antenna was out of the water, Shepard sent the
message that the whole country was waiting to hear:
". . . everything A-O.K."

A Marine helicopter had been hovering near the spot
where the capsule landed. Its pilot called Shepard on
the radio to say the helicopter was above the capsule
and ready to hook on. There was a thud as the hook
caught the top of the capsule.

"O.K.," the pilot called, "you've got two minutes to
come out."

Water was still washing over the porthole and Shepard didn't want a wave to come bursting through the
hatch when he opened it.

"Can you bring me up a bit?" he asked.

The capsule rose in the water.

"I'll be out in thirty seconds."

Shepard removed his helmet and took a last look
around Freedom 7. It was a good capsule and had
done its job well. He opened the hatch, pulled himself
through, and slipped into the sling which the helicopter
had lowered for him. He rode in the sling up to the
helicopter, which then took him to the *Lake Champlain*,
the flagship of the Space Capsule Recovery Task Force.

The helicopter also carried the Freedom 7 to the *Lake Champlain*.

America's first voyage into space was over. Her first spaceman had reached a height of 116.5 miles. He had landed safely in the ocean 302 miles from Cape Canaveral. His trip to space and back had taken just 15 minutes.

II. WHY DO WE EXPLORE SPACE?

Space begins at the outside edges of the earth's atmosphere and extends on and on endlessly. There is no exact place where space starts because the earth's atmosphere gets thinner gradually. Space could be said to begin where there is not enough oxygen to keep a man alive, or where there is no longer enough atmosphere to support an airplane. Or it could begin where there is not a trace of the earth's atmosphere left. For purposes of exploration, many scientists think of space as beginning about 20 miles above the earth's surface. Only one per cent of the earth's atmosphere is above this point and it is very thin indeed.

Space is vast, but it is not empty. It contains meteors, cosmic rays, and various forms of electromagnetic radiation. It contains the solar system of which the earth is a part—nine planets revolving around the sun. There are thousands of smaller bodies moving within this solar system.

Our sun is only one star in a vast galaxy of 200 billion stars. And there are billions of galaxies in the dis-

tant reaches of space. It is no wonder that the possibility of exploring space has intrigued men for hundreds of years.

From the beginning of history, men have been studying the stars. The Hebrews, the Egyptians, the Greeks, and other ancient peoples left behind written accounts of what they thought the universe was like. But they, and those that lived hundreds of years later, could learn no more about the stars than what they could see by gazing upward on a clear night.

All this was changed when the telescope was invented. This wonderful device which uses lenses to form enlarged images of distant objects came to us from Holland. According to one story the children of a Dutch spectacle-maker were playing in his shop one day. On his workbench were several lenses all polished and ready to be put into frames for spectacles. One of the children picked up two of the lenses and looked through them both at once. He looked at the clock on a church tower down the street. To his surprise the clock was magnified; he could see it easily. His father looked through the two lenses and realized that it was an important discovery. In the year 1608 the Dutch government gave the spectacle-maker, whose name was Hans Lippershey, 900 florins for his invention of the telescope.

News of the telescope spread rapidly throughout Europe. In Italy an astronomer and physicist named Galileo heard about it. He was a very clever man and soon had made a telescope of his own. In 1609 he looked at the sky through a telescope for the first time. He saw things that had never been seen before. He discovered that the Milky Way was made up of stars. He saw the moons of the planet Jupiter, the spots on the sun, and the mountainous surface of the moon.

Since Galileo's day telescopes have become much more powerful, and we can see farther and better with them. With cameras we can take pictures to study later. And now we have radio telescopes to help us learn about the radiations coming from objects in space.

As wonderful as these telescopes are, they can tell us about space only as it is seen through the earth's atmosphere, which we know distorts and obscures much that we want to see. In order to observe more clearly, scientists have been using rockets to send sensitive equipment high above the earth where there is little or no dust and vapor. The scientific instruments carried aloft in these space probes have provided a great amount of important new data. But scientists still want to know much more about space. And the things they want to know can best be learned if a man is sent up there to collect the information, analyze the findings, and describe what he has observed.

To send a man into space is much more difficult than to send up a collection of instruments. Man is constructed to live in the earth's atmosphere, not in space where there is no air for him to breathe, no food for him to eat, no gravity to give him stability. The extreme temperatures in space can either roast or freeze him to death. For man, space is a dark, soundless, hostile environment. It contains harmful forms of radiation from which he must be protected. And he must be protected from the meteors and the many smaller particles that abound in space.

Obviously, for his space traveling, man needs some sort of a protective capsule which will shield him and provide an environment in which he can live. And the capsule must be strong enough to withstand the tremendous speed and pressure needed to lift it and its human passenger up through the earth's atmosphere and into space. The rockets we have today—and those we will have in the foreseeable future—must travel very fast in order to get out of the earth's atmosphere before their fuel is used up. The trip from the launching pad up into space is more than a man can survive unless he is well protected from the effects of the rapid upward movement.

In space the capsule will have to supply him with all the necessities of life. Oxygen and pressurization are two vital requirements. At sea level the pressure of the air is almost 15 pounds per square inch. Approximately 21 per cent of it is oxygen, 78 per cent is nitrogen, and the rest is made up of argon and other gases. To do his best work and to be most comfortable, a man must have approximately the same pressure inside his sealed space capsule, as well as a supply of oxygen. Oxygen could be carried from the earth in tanks; it could be produced in the capsule. Or used oxygen could be recovered and then used over and over again.

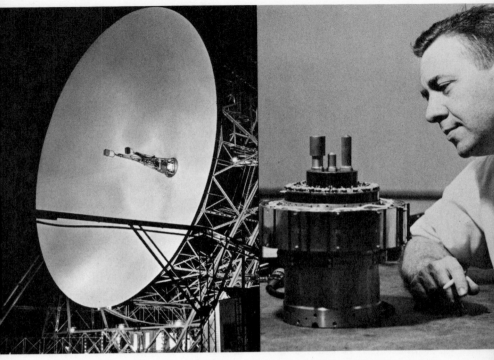

Left. *The giant reflector bowl of the Jodrell Bank radio tele-scope in England is 250 feet in diameter and weighs 750 tons.* Right. *Dr. James A. Van Allen examines the special equipment to be included in Pioneer IV for radiation detection.*

Equally important, the carbon dioxide, which is exhaled at about the same rate that oxygen is inhaled, must be removed from the capsule along with other waste materials.

Another problem is that of temperature. The side of the space capsule facing the sun will become unbearably hot from absorbing the sun's rays. But the side away from the sun will remain ice cold. If the spaceman is to be kept alive, his capsule must have an efficient air-conditioning system.

The traveler in space will also need to carry his food with him. If he is going to be in space for more than a short time, he will have to eat things that keep well and have little bulk. The problem of food supply will be complicated by the fact that both the spaceman and what he eats will be weightless once they are beyond the gravitational pull of the earth. Some of his food will be in liquid form, but most of it will consist of dehydrated or freeze-dried items to which he will add water.

Weightlessness is something we don't know very much about. We have discovered that for some people it is a pleasant experience. Others become ill with something like seasickness. During periods of weightlessness, up and down become confused and movements are difficult to control. Until a spaceman has experienced a really long period of weightlessness in flight, we can only guess at how much of a problem it will be. However, the first American astronauts to go into orbit have apparently suffered no ill effects from weightlessness during their space flights.

Another potential problem for the space traveler is loneliness and a feeling of being isolated from the earth. Some scientists think that he may become "space happy" in a very short period of time. The effects of isolation have been studied by placing volunteers in rooms resembling the interior of a spaceship. In some cases the tests have been made in complete darkness. But the people being tested know they are safely on earth and not hurtling through space, so we still don't know for sure what will happen. The first long space trip will tell us a great deal about this problem too.

Problems will exist outside as well as inside the space capsule. Ultraviolet rays, x-rays, and other forms of radiation abound in space, and protection from them must be provided. Radiation seems to be concentrated in two zones roughly 2,300 miles and 11,000 miles from the earth's surface. They are separated by a region called the "slot," where radiation is at a minimum. The two radiation zones are called the Van Allen belts in honor of the physicist, Dr. James A. Van Allen. He was responsible for the instruments which, when sent aloft in January, 1958, first detected the two regions of intense radiation.

Even if the spaceship were heavily shielded from the harmful effects of radiation, it would have no protection from collision with a meteor. Some scientists feel that there aren't enough large meteors in space for this to be a problem, but just one collision with a meteor would demolish a space craft. And space is full of small particles called micrometeors. Continuous bombardment by

micrometeors will eventually cause enough da~
hinder the operation of the spaceship.

Man's further exploration of space is certai~
going to be easy. The important question is: W
increased knowledge be worth the considerable
required to obtain it? Scientists say that the answ
yes. The knowledge that we gain about space ca~
used to greatly benefit mankind.

Weather forecasting has already become more accurate through the use of weather satellites traveling
around the earth. Communication satellites have made
world-wide television possible, and they will be able to
relay our ever growing number of transoceanic messages. Other satellites will make navigation easier for
ships and planes. Also, from space we will get a better
picture of the shape and structure of the earth. In this
way we will be able to make our maps more accurate.

These things can all be done by satellites without a
human crew. Their operations can be controlled from
the earth. But there is a limit to what can be done
without a man on the spot, using his ability to observe,
to reason, and to cope with the unexpected. Manned
space laboratories will be able to carry out a wide range
of investigation in many fields.

The important long-term benefits of space exploration
lie in increased knowledge of our universe. Man has always been an explorer of the unknown, and space is one
of the few areas still waiting to be explored. The un-
raveling of its mysteries may produce changes greater
than anything mankind has yet known.

III. SPACE EXPLORATION BEGINS

For many years we could do no more than study space with our telescopes, because there was no way to get up beyond the atmosphere. The modern rocket has changed all that. Rockets can be made powerful enough to hurl objects hundreds of miles away from the earth.

The rocket is not a new thing—the Chinese were using them as early as A.D. 1232. The Chinese already knew about gunpowder. And they discovered that, when a tube of gunpowder was fastened to the shaft of an arrow and ignited, the arrow would dart out, spreading fire as it went. Although they did not realize it, the Chinese had discovered the principle of rocket propulsion. The gases expelled by the burning gunpowder sent the arrow to its target.

In the seventeenth century Sir Isaac Newton, an English mathematician, became interested in the study of motion. He worked out three laws, or rules, that explained why things moved. The first of Newton's laws of motion states that a body remains at rest or in motion unless it is acted upon by some outside force. The

second law states that the force acting upon this body
will cause it to move in the direction of the force. And
the third law says that to every action there is an equal
and opposite reaction.

It is Newton's third law that explains what makes a
rocket shoot up into space. As fuel burns within the
rocket, gases are produced which push against the
rocket. The rocket, in turn, pushes the gases backward.
In doing so, it moves forward.

Just as the Chinese were the first to develop rockets,
they were the first to try to use them for flight. About
the year A.D. 1500, a Chinese adventurer named Wan-
Hoo fastened a chair between two kites. Behind the
chair he attached 47 gunpowder rockets. Wan-Hoo
climbed into his chair, his servants lit the rockets, and
—*whoosh!*—he was gone. No trace of Wan-Hoo or his
rocket chair was ever found.

In spite of Wan-Hoo's pioneering effort to use rockets
for flight, or perhaps because of it, the rocket continued
to be used as a military weapon almost exclusively.
During the War of 1812 the British used powerful
rockets to attack Fort McHenry near Baltimore, Maryland. Among those who saw the rockets fall on Fort
McHenry was Francis Scott Key. When he wrote our
national anthem he mentioned "the rocket's red glare."

By the end of the nineteenth century, however, there
were several proposed plans for building rocket ships.
And in 1903 a Russian schoolteacher named Konstantin
Ziolkovsky wrote a very good description of space travel
with rockets. His studies had convinced him that with

During the War of 1812 British rockets bombarded Fort Mc-Henry near Baltimore.

liquid-fuel rockets it would be possible to travel beyond the atmosphere. Ziolkovsky wrote papers in which he described the results of his study and experiments. He sent these articles to scientific societies. Unfortunately his work received little attention. It was not until after World War I that a growing interest in rocketry brought him recognition and some help from the Russian government.

By the time Konstantin Ziolkovsky died in 1935, he had become a national hero. His writings have been reprinted, and a crater on the moon has been named for him. The Soviet government refers to Ziolkovsky as the "Father of Space Travel."

America's first rocket expert was a physics professor named Robert H. Goddard. He was born in 1882 and grew up in Boston, Massachusetts. Like Konstantin Ziolkovsky, Robert Goddard became interested in the use of liquid-fuel rockets for space travel. He too was convinced that space travel was possible. Unlike Ziolkovsky, Goddard was able to transform his theories about rockets into reality. On March 16, 1926, from a snow-covered field in Auburn, Massachusetts, he successfully fired the world's first liquid-fueled rocket. It shot up to a height of 184 feet in 2½ seconds. Goddard went on to develop a pump capable of supplying the liquid fuel at a rapid rate and a gyroscope device to guide rockets in flight. He continued to improve his rockets until in 1935 he was able to send one to a height of 7,500 feet.

Before that experiment, however, neighbors' complaints about the noise of Dr. Goddard's rockets had

Left. *Robert Goddard beside his first successful liquid-fuel rocket.* Right. *A Goddard rocket in flight near Roswell, New Mexico, in 1937.*

forced him to move to the southwestern part of the
United States. At Roswell, New Mexico, where there
were few people to be bothered and ideal conditions
for testing, he carried on his rocket experiments until
his death in 1945.

In the years before World War II, Dr. Goddard's
work was almost unnoticed. Very few people in the
United States were interested in rockets. Rockets were
just something to read about in science-fiction stories.
But in far-off Silesia a young German named Wernher
von Braun heard about Dr. Goddard and his work with
rockets. Wernher wanted to become a rocket scientist
too, and he read everything he could find about rockets.
Rocketry was a popular subject in Germany. News-
papers and magazines carried stories about high-altitude rockets, rocket cars, and trips to the moon.

One day Wernher met Hermann Oberth, the most
famous of the German rocket scientists. Soon he was
working with Oberth on rocket experiments in his spare
time. He joined the German rocket society called *Ver-
ein für Raumschiffahrt* (which in English means Society
for Space Travel). The members of the society conducted
rocket experiments at a field near Berlin.

By 1932 Germany was seriously considering the development of the rocket for use as a powerful weapon.
The army offered to send young von Braun to the University of Berlin to study physics. In addition he would
be allowed to use army facilities for rocket experiments.
Von Braun accepted the offer, and for two years he was

a student at the university. When he received his degree he was immediately given the job of developing a military rocket. What the army wanted was a really big rocket, one that could travel 160 miles at a top speed of 3,350 miles an hour. It was to carry one ton of explosives in its nose. To build it, the leading German rocket experts were gathered together and put to work at a place called Peenemuende on the Baltic sea coast.

Wernher von Braun played a leading part in developing this rocket, which came to be known as the V-2. It was fired for the first time in October, 1942, three years after the outbreak of World War II. The test shot was a success, and the Germans began to build the sites from which they planned to launch their powerful rocket against Great Britain.

All did not go smoothly, however. British bombers dropped tons of bombs on Peenemuende. And von Braun was arrested by the Gestapo and charged with treason. He was released when it became apparent that V-2 production could not proceed without him, but precious time had been lost.

The first V-2s were fired against the British on September 8, 1944. Unlike the earlier V-1 "flying bomb," which was an aerial torpedo with wings and very noisy, the V-2 descended on its target without a sound. The slightly more than 1,000 V-2s that fell on Great Britain killed 2,855 people and seriously injured 6,268 more. In addition there was considerable damage to buildings. If

the V-2 had been ready earlier, it might have altered
the course of the war. But it came too late. By January, 1945, the Russian army was so close to Peenemuende that the rocket experts were forced to flee. They decided to go to where they could surrender to the Americans. With some difficulty they made their way to Reutte, Austria, in the Bavarian Alps. There they waited until the Americans were near.

Because Wernher's brother, Magnus, spoke the best English, he was sent to find some American soldiers to surrender to. When he found them he said, "We are a group of rocket specialists up in the mountains. We want to see your commander and surrender to the Americans."

It so happened that plans had already been made for questioning the Peenemuende rocket specialists if they could be found. The project was known as "Operation Paperclip," because the cards of the most important men were marked with paper clips. There was much excitement when it was learned that many of the rocket experts had been located. Because they knew so much about rockets, a number of them were brought to the United States for questioning. A Rocket Research and Development Center was established at El Paso, Texas. And under the leadership of Wernher von Braun, the German experts went to work. They began with the assembling and launching of V-2 rockets which had been captured in Germany. These rockets carried no high explosives. Instead they were equipped with scientific instruments.

Wernher von Braun (center) and two other German scientists check a V-2 engine being readied for a test at White Sands, New Mexico, in 1946.

The United States had already begun its exploration of space with "sounding rockets." A sounding rocket is one that travels not more than 3,950 miles before falling back to the earth's surface. It carries instruments which examine the area through which the rocket is traveling. In the beginning, of course, the rockets didn't go nearly so high as 3,950 miles. One of the first American sounding rockets reached a height of 43½ miles. It was a WAC Corporal launched in 1945 from the newly established rocket-testing center at White Sands, New Mexico.

By the next year the V-2s brought from Germany had been assembled and were ready for firing. Carrying delicate scientific instruments instead of deadly explosives, they gathered information from altitudes high above the earth's surface. This information enabled scientists to check on things they had only guessed at before. One of the V-2s reached a height of 137 miles. But since the V-2 had been designed to demolish a target with a ton of high explosives, it wasn't too well suited to high-altitude research. It was eventually modified and given the name Viking.

The WAC Corporal had been too small to travel very high. It too was improved. In February, 1949, at White Sands, a WAC Corporal was mounted on a modified V-2 rocket. The V-2 carried the WAC Corporal to a height of 20 miles. Then the two rockets separated and the WAC Corporal was fired. It climbed to a record-breaking height of 250 miles, carrying 50 pounds of radio and electronic equipment. This was a very important rocket firing because it proved that a two-stage rocket was possible. By building rockets with two or more stages, or units, scientists could send them much higher than one rocket could travel alone.

These were exciting days for the workers at the White Sands Proving Ground. They were constantly learning new things about rocket design and performance. The instruments sent aloft revealed amazing facts. Scientists all over the country sent in suggestions for improving the instruments, as well as ideas for new data to be collected. There were so many things to be studied that it was difficult to decide which ones to work on first.

Once the scientists had determined which data were to be gathered by a new rocket, they had to select the instruments that would best do the job. Then these instruments had to be fitted into the small nose cone of the rocket. When a single rocket was being used to measure more than one thing, the instruments had to be placed where they would not interfere with one another. A great deal of ingenuity went into the designing of the instruments that were carried by the White Sands rockets. They had to do their work in a very small space, and they had to be as foolproof as possible so that the information they gathered would be accurate.

Of course the data collected by a sounding rocket is useful only if it can be returned to the earth. Sometimes an automatic radio transmitter sends the information to a receiver on the ground. Such a transmitter is called a telemeter. Another method is to record the data, as it is collected, on film or magnetic tape carried in the rocket. If this is done, the rocket must be recovered when it returns to earth. In the early days of sounding rockets, many hours were spent searching the desert around the White Sands Proving Ground to find rockets that had managed to elude the scientists who were tracking them. Gradually, improved methods of tracking were developed until it was possible to send living animals up in rockets and recover them unharmed when they came down.

The sounding rockets themselves were improved, too. They went higher and carried more instruments. But they were still able to record high-altitude data for only a few minutes before falling back to earth. The next step was to send a space vehicle into orbit around the earth so that it could send back continuous information on conditions in space. Such a vehicle is called an artificial earth satellite. It is launched into orbit around the earth by sending it up at a very high speed. Its speed tends to carry the satellite away from the earth; at the same time gravity keeps pulling it toward the earth. At the point where these two forces are exactly balanced, the satellite will go into orbit around the earth.

Scientists are able to figure just how fast a satellite must be traveling to go into orbit. For example, if a satellite is to be sent around the earth at a height of 200 miles, it must reach a speed of 18,000 miles an hour. On the basis of the satellite's speed, scientists can also predict whether the path it will follow will be a truly

Three Army Ordnance technicians hold a WAC Corporal rocket in a vertical position.

circular one or one that resembles a closed curve. This last type is known as an elliptical orbit and is the one followed by most satellites.

Satellites can be built in a variety of shapes and sizes. The size, shape, and amount of the equipment to be carried into space play a big part in determining what a satellite will look like. The satellite is carried aloft at the forward end of a rocket which fires in stages, each stage falling away as its fuel is used up. The last stage must carry the satellite fast enough and far enough for it to go into orbit.

Rocket experts were able to launch an earth satellite on paper long before the first one was actually sent into space. They knew how fast it would have to travel, the path it would take, and even how long it would stay in orbit.

What they were waiting for was a rocket with sufficient power to lift the satellite high enough and fast enough. They also had to work out ways of stabilizing the motion of the satellite and guiding it in flight.

The scientists of the Soviet Union were the first to solve these problems. On October 4, 1957, the Soviet Union announced that it had successfully launched the first man-made satellite. Its speed of five miles a second was carrying it around the earth once every ninety-two minutes. As it whizzed along, it transmitted a "beep-beep" signal to the world below. *Sputnik*, or "Fellow-Traveler," as the Russians called their satellite, weighed 184 pounds. It measured 23 inches in diameter, about the size of a basketball.

The launching of Sputnik I marked the true beginning of the space age, and the Soviet Union was justly proud of what it had accomplished. At the end of World War II some of the German rocket scientists had also been captured by Russian soldiers. These men went to work for the Soviet Union just as Wernher von Braun and his colleagues had gone to work for the United States. During the years that Americans were experimenting with rockets at the White Sands Proving Ground, similar experiments were going on in the Soviet Union. Sometime during those years, the scientists there learned the secret of building rockets with tremendous boosting power.

That they had done so was demonstrated on November 3, 1957, when Sputnik II was sent into orbit. It weighed 1,120 pounds. And it carried a passenger! Along with instruments for measuring cosmic rays and solar radiation, and radio transmitters to report the data to earth, rode a dog named Laika. Her reactions to her ride through space were also radioed to earth.

Since 1957 a number of satellites have been placed in orbit around the earth. Some have even been sent into orbit around the sun. While these satellites have not created quite as much excitement as the first two Sputniks, each has helped turn into reality man's dream of escaping the forces that hold him to the earth.

Explorer I, which the United States orbited in 1958, gave us our first information on the Van Allen radiation belts. A third Sputnik, also launched in 1958, measured a variety of things including cosmic rays, magnetic fields, and radiation. It also reported on meteors in space. The fourth satellite in the United States Explorer series carried out a more detailed study of radiation belts. Other satellites have sent back information on weather. They have provided a better picture of what the earth really looks like and they have carried animals, enabling us to study the effect of space travel on living things.

These unmanned satellites added greatly to our knowledge of space, but they marked just the beginning of space exploration.

IV. PROJECT MERCURY

The beep-beep of that first Sputnik, as it traveled on its orbit around the earth in the fall of 1957, caused the United States to take a new look at its own space program. Our sounding rockets had supplied us with a great deal of valuable information about space, but how close were we to putting a satellite into orbit? We had been thinking about it for years, of course. In fact we had begun thinking about it long before the necessary equipment was available.

By the summer of 1954 Wernher von Braun felt that we had at last developed rockets that could do the job. He told a group of Army and Navy officials that the Redstone missile, combined with three smaller Loki rockets, which had also been developed by the Army's Redstone Arsenal, could boost a small satellite into orbit. This was good news indeed. The Army and the Navy decided to coöperate on the project, which was called Orbiter.

Then in the summer of 1955 the United States government announced an entirely different project. It was

Project Vanguard, a satellite program to be conducted in connection with the International Geophysical Year planned for 1957. Plans for Project Vanguard called for the use of no military equipment such as the Army's Redstone missile. Work began at once on the development of an entirely new rocket. Wernher von Braun's Project Orbiter was dropped.

Project Vanguard progress was slow, however. For one thing rocket development is expensive. The $22,-000,000 that had been set aside for the project turned out to be not nearly enough, and more money was hard to get. In the mid-1950s Americans were not yet convinced of the importance of developing rockets and satellites.

In December, 1956, the first stage of the Vanguard rocket was ready for its first test. Slim and glistening, it shot out over the Atlantic at 4,000 miles an hour. That test was a complete success, but there was still much work to be done. And as time went on, problems began to appear. The Vanguard satellite shot had been scheduled for the summer of 1957; then it was postponed to late fall.

In the meantime the Russians had put the first two Sputniks into orbit. And all the world was watching to see if the United States, too, could send a satellite into orbit. Unfortunately the very next Vanguard test shot on December 6, 1957, was a dismal failure. The rocket rose a few feet and then fell back on its launching pad in flames.

Left. *The Vanguard rocket tested in December, 1957, rose only a few feet, then fell back on the launching pad in flames.* Right. *On January 31, 1958, a Jupiter-C rocket put Explorer I, America's first artificial satellite, into orbit.*

Of course it was only a test shot, and our scientists had stressed that fact. The complex second stage of the rocket had never been fired before, and a perfect shot was unlikely. But the once beautiful rocket, burning on its launching pad, dealt a severe blow to American pride.

Meanwhile, what had happened to Project Orbiter, the first plan for putting up an American satellite? It had been shelved in favor of Project Vanguard, but it hadn't been forgotten. When the first Sputnik went up, Wernher von Braun told Neil McElroy, the man who was to be the new secretary of defense: "We can fire a satellite into orbit 60 days from the moment you give us a green light!"

And he did it! On January 31, 1958, the first American satellite was sent into orbit around the earth. Von Braun used a Jupiter-C rocket, an improved version of the Redstone rocket he had planned to use in 1954. The satellite, called Explorer I, weighed only 18 pounds, much less than the Sputniks, but it was up there. And Americans had been thoroughly awakened to the importance of space exploration.

On March 17, 1958, after more disheartening failures, a six-inch Vanguard satellite was finally sent into orbit. Nine days later von Braun and his rocket experts orbited a second Explorer; in July they sent up another. And in December, a few days before Christmas, one of the Atlas intercontinental ballistic missiles developed by the Air Force was placed in orbit. This shot was called Proj-

The face of Wernher von Braun (center) reflects the tension in the blockhouse as the moment approaches to launch Explorer III into orbit.

ect SCORE, the letters standing for Signal Communication by Orbiting Relay Equipment. The two-way communications system carried by the satellite enabled it to record the human voice in outer space and then send it back to earth. One of the recorded voices was that of President Eisenhower. His Christmas message was sent up to the satellite, which taped and stored it. At a signal from the ground the satellite rebroadcast the message to the world. It said:

"This is the President of the United States speaking.

"Through the marvels of scientific advance, my voice is coming to you from a satellite traveling in outer space.

"My message is a simple one.

"Through this unique means I convey to you and to all mankind America's wish for peace on earth and good will toward men everywhere."

The accelerated schedule of satellite launchings set in motion in 1958 was part of a revised United States space program. It had been revised because the Soviet Union's Sputniks had made us realize that we had been dragging our feet in space research.

Such progress as we had made had come from a number of projects often conducted quite independently of one another. The Army had developed and tested rockets at its White Sands Proving Ground. Later it set up a Guided Missile Development Division at Huntsville, Alabama, under the direction of Wernher von Braun. Explorer I had come from Huntsville.

The Air Force was also interested in guided missiles.

It opened a testing site at Cape Canaveral, Florida, and began work on a variety of missiles, one of which was the Atlas that broadcast President Eisenhower's message. Another Air Force project was the development of supersonic, high-altitude aircraft.

The Navy was experimenting with various types of missiles, and it was responsible for Project Vanguard.

In addition to these military agencies, there was a civilian organization engaged in space research. It was the National Advisory Committee for Aeronautics which, since 1915, had been dealing with problems of flight. As planes flew higher and faster, it had extended its research to the problems of high-altitude and space flight.

President Eisenhower and his advisors became convinced that the United States would make faster progress if more of the scientists could work together to solve the problems of exploring space. In April, 1958, the President asked Congress to set up the National Aeronautics and Space Agency (NASA). This new agency was to take over the work of the National Advisory Committee for Aeronautics and be responsible for the civilian space science and exploration program.

The National Aeronautics and Space Act was passed by Congress on July 29, 1958. The act declared: "It is the policy of the United States that activities in space should be devoted to peaceful purposes for the benefit of mankind."

In October the National Aeronautics and Space Administration was established. Dr. T. Keith Glennan, the president of the Case Institute of Technology, was named administrator. From the National Advisory Committee for Aeronautics NASA inherited 8,000 employees and five research centers. These centers included the Langley Laboratory at Langley Air Force Base, Virginia, which studied aircraft and missile structures; the Ames Aeronautical Laboratory at Moffett Naval Air Station in California, which studied the problems of high-speed flight; the Lewis Flight Propulsion Laboratory at Cleveland, Ohio, which worked on engines for airplanes and spaceships; the High Speed Flight Station at Edwards Air Force Base, California, where experiments with manned rockets were under way; and Wallops Island, Virginia, which tested rocket-powered vehicles. At Greenbelt, Maryland, NASA built a sixth laboratory, the Goddard Space Flight Center, named for the rocket pioneer.

NASA's space research began at once. It took over the Vanguard project from the Navy, and the Army's Huntsville laboratories became part of NASA along with Dr. von Braun and 5,500 employees. During its first year, NASA sent three rockets loaded with instruments deep into space. It put three new satellites into orbit. It worked with the rocket-powered X-15 aircraft and conducted tests with new rockets and satellites.

All this was part of NASA's broad research and development program aimed at furthering the exploration of space, first with unmanned and then with manned space vehicles. Their complete schedule called for exploration at an ever increasing distance from the earth —first to the moon, then to the planets Mars and Venus, and finally to the outer planets. The important first step, the achievement upon which NASA's entire program depended, was the placing of a manned space capsule into orbit around the earth. This became NASA's Project Mercury. Project Mercury would open the way to the moon and the planets.

In the fall of 1958 a group of engineers and scientists received the most challenging, and the most interesting, assignment to come out of the new space age. Their job was to send a manned space capsule into orbit around the earth, study the man's ability to live and work in space, and then return the man and the capsule safely back to earth. The engineers and scientists were members of the Space Task Group which the new National Aeronautics and Space Administration organized when just four days old. Under the direction of Robert R. Gilruth, the Space Task Group was to work on NASA's vitally important Project Mercury.

The men of the Space Task Group were well chosen for the tremendous challenge that lay ahead of them. For some time they had been studying the problems of space flight at the Langley Aeronautical and Lewis Flight Propulsion laboratories. Even though there had been no immediate prospect of sending a man into space, they had made a start at getting him there.

Serious work on plans for space flight had gotten under way in the United States early in 1956. At that time the Air Force began studying the problem of recovering a manned space capsule after it had been sent into orbit around the earth. The Air Force also began to develop space capsules that could be used for preliminary tests with animals.

The Army worked out a plan for sending a manned space capsule up about 150 miles, using the Redstone rocket. Recovery was to be by parachute. The Navy proposed sending a man into orbit in a collapsible pneumatic glider. The glider was to be launched in the nose of a giant rocket. Once in orbit, the glider would be inflated and flown down to a water landing by its pilot.

At the same time the men who were to form the Space Task Group were working on the many problems involved in putting a manned satellite into orbit. They worked on the best design for a space capsule and the development of a more powerful booster rocket.

All this study and planning for space flight had been carried on with very little money and no definite program for putting a man into space. But scientists were sure it would be done eventually, so they had gone ahead with some of the preliminary work. Then came the successful launching of the Soviet Sputnik. Suddenly, putting a man into space became the most important project of the newly established National Aeronautics and Space Administration. To get the program into operation, the agency was allotted $46,416,330 for research and development expenses and $2,425,000 for construction and equipment. Things were moving ahead at last!

Top. *Robert R. Gilruth (second from right), first director of the Space Task Group, conducts a news conference. With him (left to right) are Virgil Grissom, Rear Admiral John Chew, and Walter C. Williams.* Bottom. *A huge Atlas rocket leaves the assembly line in San Diego, California. After final checkout, it will be flown to Cape Canaveral.*

The men of the Space Task Group went to work at the Langley Research Center. Their objective was to put a man into orbit around the earth as soon as possible, but not before it was safe for him to go. They intended to make orbital flight no more risky than testing a new type of airplane.

The many factors involved in a successful space flight were divided among the members of the Space Task Group. Some worked on the problems of launching and recovery. Others were concerned with the rocket boosters, others with the numerous things that had to go into a space capsule to make sure its passenger survived his trip. To help them the members of the group had the advice of doctors who had specialized in space medicine. They could also call on the rest of NASA, the armed services, the universities, and industry. Project Mercury was the United States' first step toward interplanetary space flight. The lessons learned from its successful execution would determine what we could do next and how soon we could do it. Everyone was willing to help.

How long would it take for Project Mercury to put a man into orbit around the earth? The Space Task Group couldn't say for sure. To save time they planned to make as much use as possible of the equipment already available. They would use the Air Force's Atlas missile to boost their capsule up into space. (The Atlas was the only missile the United States had developed that was powerful enough to do the job.) To get their capsule into and out of orbit, they would use the simplest method that could be relied on to work. But they would still have to proceed slowly and carefully.

The men of the Space Task Group knew that they weren't the only ones working on the problem of putting a man into orbit around the earth. The scientists of the Soviet Union were doing the same thing. Although the United States naturally wanted to be the first to achieve manned space flight, Project Mercury was based on the fact that the safety of the astronaut was of the utmost importance. The Space Task Group could take no short cuts that might endanger the astronaut's life. Everything that went into Project Mercury would be tested over and over again.

A great many things were going into Project Mercury. There was the space capsule to be lifted high above the earth by an Atlas launch vehicle. After the capsule had circled the earth three times, it would have to be slowed down and returned to earth. All this would be accomplished while radio contact was being maintained with the capsule and a vast tracking network following its flight. Once the capsule began to descend, ships and planes would have to watch for it.

The object of all this care and attention, the man inside the capsule, would have to be protected in every way possible from the hostile space environment through which he traveled. In case something went wrong, he would have to be snatched from his capsule. If all went well, the effects of his journey would be studied with greatest care. From launch to landing his reactions would be recorded. In that way the Space Task Group would learn things to help prepare for future space flights. And, finally, detailed plans would have to be made for picking up the astronaut very quickly when he landed, because he would be coming down in the Atlantic Ocean.

Although these problems seemed to be enough to keep the members of the Space Task Group busy for a long, long time, they hoped Project Mercury would take no more than two or three years to put a man into orbit around the earth and bring him back.

V. THE EQUIPMENT FOR
   EXPLORING SPACE

"It looks like a big television tube!" That's what was said most often about the Project Mercury space capsule developed to carry a man around the earth. Tailored to fit the Atlas missile, it wasn't very large—only six feet across at its wide end and ten feet long. But it was strong. Its double walls could stand up under the stress of accelerating to a speed of 18,000 miles an hour. Friction heat up to 2,000 degrees didn't melt them.

The immense amount of heat that would be generated when a space craft reëntered the earth's atmosphere was the biggest problem faced by space-capsule designers. Aerodynamic experts began by experimenting with the streamlined shapes which worked well with high-speed aircraft. But when these sleek, needle-nosed shapes were used for space vehicles, they promptly burned up when they met the friction of the earth's atmosphere on the return trip. Streamlining reduced air resistance, but it also seemed to trap heat along the sides of the vehicle. A space craft, traveling much faster than an airplane, trapped so much heat that it burned.

It was NASA aerodynamics expert, H. Julien Allen, who solved the problem. He reasoned that a streamlined shape was the worst possible one for a space capsule. It should be exactly the opposite—blunt or stubby. Then heat would be bounced back into the atmosphere in the form of shock waves instead of collecting along the sides of the capsule. Allen's idea worked so well that a blunt shape became standard for space vehicles.

As a further protection against heat, a special shield was built over the blunt end of the Mercury capsule. The shield was coated with a resinous glass fiber which vaporized when it got hot, carrying away heat in the process.

The blunt end of the capsule served still another purpose. It helped to slow the capsule down on its return journey. Eighteen thousand miles an hour is much too fast for a landing!

Opposite the blunt end of the capsule, in the narrow top portion, were stored the parachutes used in landing. A small chute called a drogue opened at 21,000 feet and a larger one lowered the capsule the rest of the way, landing it on the water as gently as possible. There was a third reserve chute in case it was needed. This is an example of the way much of the capsule's equipment was duplicated as an extra safeguard for the astronaut.

Towering above the capsule was the escape system. Booster rockets, such as the Atlas, were getting progressively more reliable, but every now and then something did go wrong. A rocket could blow up on the launching pad, or go off course, or fail to reach the right altitude.

Top. *H. Julien Allen, the aerodynamics expert who conceived of a blunt-shaped capsule.* Bottom. *View of a Mercury space capsule showing the escape rocket atop the spaceship.*

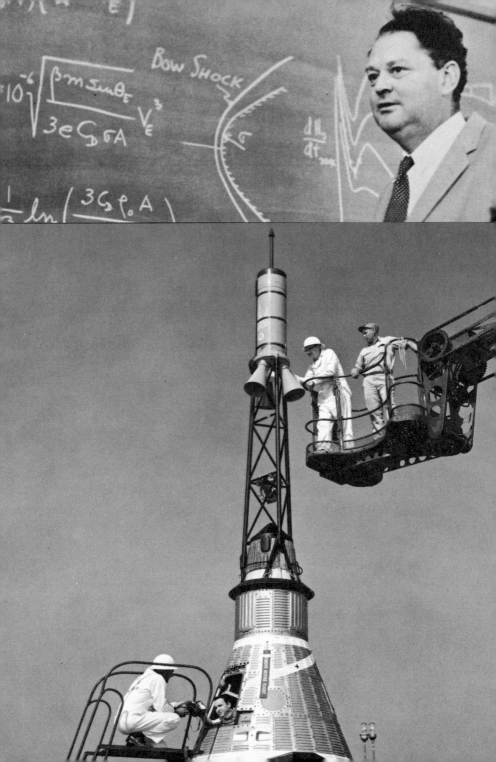

What would happen to the astronaut then? He must end his space flight in a hurry! His capsule would be blasted clear of the malfunctioning booster rocket by another, smaller rocket mounted in a 16-foot, orange-colored tower attached to the top of the capsule.

The escape rocket was a powerful, solid-fuel-burning device that could lift the capsule 2,500 feet into the air. It lifted it, not straight up, but slightly to one side so that it would be clear of the malfunctioning rocket below.

The key to a successful escape is speedy action. An electronic watch was kept on the booster rocket. If anything went wrong, an automatic signal would go out to the escape rocket, which then lifted the capsule out of the danger area. If the automatic firing system didn't work, the men monitoring the launching could start the escape rocket on its way. If all else failed, the astronaut himself could push a switch and start the escape procedure. He would have only a few seconds, but the system was designed to work quickly. A series of clamps holding the capsule to the booster snapped open. The escape rocket fired, and the capsule was up and away from the danger area. When a safe altitude was reached, a parachute lowered the capsule back to earth.

The important part of the capsule was the enclosure, or cockpit, for the astronaut. It was small; there was just enough room for the astronaut and all the instruments needed to keep track of him and his space craft.

The entire bottom of the capsule—the six-foot, blunt end—was occupied by the astronaut's couch. This was a fiber-glass and foam-rubber support especially designed to help the astronaut withstand the strains of launching and reëntry into the earth's atmosphere.

The instrument panel was located directly in front of the astronaut as he lay strapped to his couch. He could also use a periscope or look out of a small window without moving his head. There were times during flight when it would be difficult, or even impossible, for him to move more than his eyes. The capsule control stick was located near his right hand. The motion of the capsule could be directed with this one, single-hand control.

The capsule's door was a small hatch through which the astronaut had to crawl. Once he was inside and the hatch was sealed, the atmosphere in the capsule was pressurized, cooled, and dehumidified.

As complicated and as wonderful as the Mercury capsule was, it was developed in a very short time. From the studies that had already been made of space vehicles, the new NASA Space Task Group had a good idea of what would be needed. Within a matter of weeks the McDonnell Aircraft Corporation had signed a contract to design, build, and develop a capsule for the Space Task Group.

Every part of the capsule was tested and tested again. Small-scale models were observed in wind tunnels and during flight. McDonnell turned out full-size "boilerplate" models made of sheet metal, which were used to test the various capsule mechanisms. Sometimes everything worked as it should, and sometimes

there was failure. Then the Space Task Group and Mc-
Donnell technicians would have to figure out what went
wrong and try again.

One of the most spectacular failures, for those who
were watching, was the November, 1960, test firing in
which the rocket lifted off the launching pad and then
dropped back. Within seconds the air was filled with
parachutes, smoke, and flame as the capsule's parachutes were released and its escape rocket fired.

It was discovered later that a malfunction had shut
off the booster rocket's engines just as it was leaving
the launching pad. The escape rocket received the same
signal it would have received if the booster had exhausted its fuel in space and shut down on schedule, so
the escape rocket fired just as it would have done miles
above the earth. But since the capsule was surrounded
by air instead of space, another control device released
the parachutes which would have eased its descent
through the atmosphere. All this time the capsule,
sending out the signals and flashing the lights that
would be used during a normal descent, was still sit-
ting on the launching pad.

Test failures such as this delayed Project Mercury for
days and weeks until everything that went wrong could
be located and corrected. But each correction made the
men of the Space Task Group all the more certain that
everything would work perfectly when an astronaut finally rode in the Mercury capsule.

The Atlas missile chosen to boost the Mercury capsule
into orbit was developed by the Air Force as an inter-

*Top. Technicians subject a new capsule to hundreds of hours
of careful checkout procedures. Bottom. A Mercury capsule
is lowered onto an Atlas rocket in preparation for a test firing.*

continental ballistic missile or ICBM. A ballistic missile
is one that contains pre-set controls which keep it on
its course. A guided missile, on the other hand, is controlled by radio from the ground. All missiles are propelled by rocket engines, and the term "rocket" is often
used to designate the entire missile.

The Atlas had three powerful engines. Two were boosters that blasted for 150 seconds after being ignited. They
then dropped off and the third engine continued. The
three engines developed a combined total of 360,000
pounds of thrust. The Redstone rocket used in some of
the Mercury test firings delivered a thrust of only 78,000
pounds, not enough to put the ton-and-a-half Mercury
capsule into orbit. It was the Atlas' third stage that lifted
the capsule to the proper altitude for orbit.

The Atlas was more than 70 feet high. That made it
taller than an average seven-story building. It was about
ten feet in diameter. This sounds big, but all the space
was needed. Inside its frame the missile carried fuel tanks
for kerosene and liquid oxygen, a complicated system of
fuel controls and tubes, and a guidance system capable
of directing it to a point as much as 9,000 miles away.

Work on the Atlas, which was manufactured by General
Dynamics Astronautics, began in 1951. But the missile
wasn't fired with any great success until 1958, the year
it was used to broadcast the President's Christmas message. It became operational, or ready for use as a weapon
by the Air Force, in the fall of 1958.

There was a whole family of Atlas missiles—the Atlas-

Able, the Atlas-Agena-A, the Atlas-Agena-B, the Atlas Centaur, and the Atlas-D. Designed for different purposes, they had the same first stage, but their second- and third-stage rockets differed. The one chosen for Project Mercury, the Atlas-D, had undergone more testing than the others because of the nature of its mission. The Atlas had thousands of parts, any one of which could go wrong, so not all the tests were successful. The performance of the Atlas-D had been good enough, however, to win the confidence of the men chosen to ride it up into space.

A big part of Project Mercury never left the ground. The Space Task Group had to arrange for a vast array of people and instruments to watch over the launching of the capsule, its flight around the earth, and finally its landing in the Atlantic.

A control center was set up at Cape Canaveral, where the Mercury launchings were to take place. The men assigned there, all Mercury experts, would decide when the countdown should begin, when it should be held up, and even if the space shot should be called off altogether. They would follow the launching carefully, using television and instrument readings to check on what was happening to the Atlas, the capsule, and the astronaut. Once the capsule went into orbit they would continue to follow its progress and to talk with the astronaut by radio.

The Space Task Group also had to arrange for other groups of experts to monitor the Mercury capsule's

At the Cape Canaveral Control Center the orbital flight tracking stations are plotted on an enormous board.

flight along the path it would follow as it circled the earth. This was the tracking network set up so that at no time on his journey would the man in the capsule be out of contact with men on the earth. At some of the 18 tracking stations there had to be equipment to bring the capsule down in case of trouble. All of them had to be able to track the capsule, collect information about it, and communicate with the astronaut. In addition to Cape Canaveral, Project Mercury tracking stations were planned for Bermuda, the Canary Islands, a ship in the Atlantic, two places in Africa, a ship in the Indian Ocean, two places in Australia, Canton Island in the Pacific Ocean, Hawaii, Southern California, Mexico, New Mexico, Texas, and an air base in Florida. Two additional stations on Grand Bahama and Grand Turk islands in the Atlantic would track the capsule during launching and recovery.

Finally, the Space Task Group had to plan for the successful recovery of the capsule and the astronaut from the Atlantic when the flight was over. Arrangements were made to have ships, airplanes, and helicopters deployed in all the places where the landing might take place—many of them in the area where the landing was planned and fewer where a landing was less likely. The recovery planes and ships had to be equipped with radar and other devices for locating the capsule. The capsule itself was to be equipped with a radio, yellow water dyes, smoke flares, and depth charges to attract the attention of searchers.

As much care went into the development of the

earth-bound portion of Project Mercury as went into the capsule. The Control Center, the tracking network, and the recovery forces would play an important part in bringing the astronaut back alive. And Project Mercury definitely intended to bring him back safely.

VI. CHOOSING THE
MERCURY ASTRONAUT

MEN WANTED FOR TRAINING PROGRAM. *Must be gradu-*
ates of military test pilot school with at least 1,500 hours
flying experience. Bachelor degree or equivalent in en-
gineering or science required. Under 40 years of age
and not more than 5 feet, 11 inches tall.

This ad never appeared, but it lists some of the requirements NASA's Space Task Group drew up for the man
who was going to take that all-important first trip into
space.

Just what would make a good spaceman? That was a
difficult question for Project Mercury officials to answer.
There were no spacemen to study for good and bad
qualities. And no one knew for sure just what would be
required of a spaceman as he traveled around the earth.
One thing was certain—he would have to be a man
willing to face the unknown and able to deal with any
problems it might present.

The Space Task Group didn't have much time to decide what kind of a man to look for and where to find

him. As soon as Project Mercury got under way in the fall of 1958, it was imperative that a group of astronauts be selected and their training begun. They were going to do more than ride in the completed capsule; they were going to have a big part in the development of the Mercury program.

Beyond a doubt there were thousands of young men in the United States who would make good spacemen. The problem was to find those who would make the *best* spacemen and find them as quickly as possible. They would be the ones in the best physical condition; they would have the best mental attitude toward space flight; and they would have the best technical background.

One special group of men seemed to be a good source from which to choose. They were the nation's military test pilots. They had the necessary engineering training and experience with fast, high-flying aircraft. As test pilots they had already demonstrated that they could perform under difficult conditions.

Not all the test pilots in the United States are in the Air Force, Navy, or Marine Corps. Some very good ones test new planes and new equipment for aircraft companies. The Space Task Group, however, decided to consider only military test pilots because they could be easily transferred to Project Mercury. Their regular pay and allowances would continue, and they were already accustomed to a military way of life. And, an important point, complete records on them were available for Project Mercury officials.

As a test pilot, John Glenn made a record flight from California to New York (3 hours, 23 minutes, 8.4 seconds) while trying out an F8FU Crusader jet on March 9, 1955.

Hundreds of these records were examined by an NASA selection board late in 1958. Some basic requirements had already been settled. The men chosen could be no more than 5 feet, 11 inches tall. The size of the capsule made this rule necessary. The selection board also agreed that 1,500 hours of flying time would produce an experienced pilot, and they felt that the educational requirements must provide for the necessary technical background.

The records were studied with the greatest care. When the job was finished in January, 1959, one hundred and ten men had survived the initial screening. The main reason for elimination was lack of enough technical experience. Even so, the selection was difficult. The test pilots were an extremely well-qualified group of men.

An even more difficult selection lay ahead. For out of the initial 110 must be chosen the very best of the best. The men were divided into three groups for personal interviews.

The pilots came to Washington from all over the country. Their travel orders didn't tell them very much, but they soon found out what the trip was all about. They were thoroughly briefed on Project Mercury— what it had already done, what it hoped to do. Then they were asked, "Would you like to volunteer to be the man Project Mercury will send into space?"

It was expected that not every pilot would say yes, and not all of them did. Some were already deeply involved in important projects they didn't want to leave. Some had other reasons for saying no. The amazing thing, however, was the number who did say yes. Of the first 69 pilots who were asked, no less than 55 volunteered for Project Mercury.

With so many highly qualified candidates on hand there was no need to call in the rest of the 110 test pilots. In fact the number of candidates had to be reduced to 32. This was done through a series of interviews and advanced aptitude tests. The men were questioned about their knowledge of engineering, their military background, their childhood, their likes and dislikes. Once again the very best of the best were chosen.

But even 32 highly qualified men were more than Project Mercury could use. It had been decided to limit the final selection to seven. Then each one could be assigned a different part of the Mercury program as an area of specialization. A final series of tests would have to reduce the 32 to 7.

The tests began at the Lovelace Clinic in Albuquerque, New Mexico. In groups of six or seven the thirty-two candidates went to Albuquerque where they were given the most thorough physical examinations possible. For seven and one-half days they were probed and prodded. They were x-rayed, their brain waves measured, their eyes were examined. They were immersed in a tank of water so their specific gravity could be determined. Their hearts, circulatory systems, stomachs, muscles, bones, and glands were all checked with the greatest care. Since they were test pilots, all of these men were naturally required to be in good physical condition. The doctors were looking for those who were in the very best physical condition.

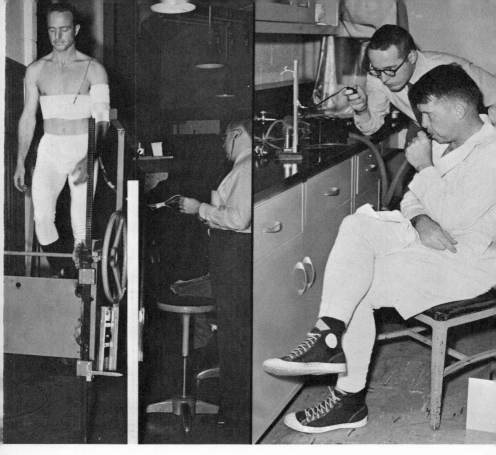

Left. *Navy Lieutenant Scott Carpenter walks a treadmill as part of his heart test.* Right. *To measure his lung capacity, Walter Schirra blows through a hose to see how long he can hold up the column of mercury in the tube at left.*

Albuquerque was only the beginning. From the Lovelace Clinic the candidates went to Wright Patterson Air Force Base at Dayton, Ohio. There they underwent another series of tests—this time to measure how well they performed under stress. Not one of these tests was very comfortable. The men had to spend two hours in a heat chamber with the temperature at 130 degrees Fahrenheit. They were spun around in a centrifuge, placed in a pressure chamber, in a dark soundproof room, in an ice bath. They walked on treadmills, rode on tilt tables, stepped up twenty inches to a platform every two seconds for five minutes.

During these tests the candidates were studied to see how well they performed in difficult or confusing situations. Then they moved on to the last series of tests— psychological, intelligence, and aptitude. In this part of the screening process they took a "self-inventory" examination in which they answered 566 questions about themselves. They were also interviewed by psychiatrists and took several standard written tests.

When it was all over, the exhausted candidates went home. They were, without a doubt, the most tested men that ever lived, and the Project Mercury selection board was faced with the task of evaluating the results of all those tests.

The half-dozen men on the board were all medical or technical experts. The candidates were unknown to them. From the beginning, numbers had been used instead of the names of the men being considered. The final selection would be based strictly on the records now before the board.

It would have been easy to choose more than seven men. The results of the tests showed that many of the candidates were truly superior, both mentally and physically. The choice of only seven was a difficult one. Once again it was a matter of picking the very best from a group of highly qualified individuals. It was important that no possible flaw in any of the candidates be overlooked. The success of Project Mercury would depend on the seven who were chosen.

In general, what were the men like whose records were before the Project Mercury selection board? Their ages ranged from 28 to 38; all were married. Only two had lived in large cities before going to college, and 20 were only, or eldest, children. They were comfortable, mature, adaptable men with lots of drive. They were intelligent. Their intelligence scores ranged from 130 to 141 (a score of 100 is average).

Most of the candidates had entered military service during World War II. Their attitudes toward flying varied. Some of them had wanted to fly from an early age; others had had the average boy's interest in airplanes. About half of the group had volunteered for test-pilot training. The rest had been selected for the job because of their accomplishments in some other field. They did not consider their work unduly dangerous. For them, knowledge and caution were a big part of safe flying.

Their reasons for volunteering for Project Mercury? They considered it an important undertaking and wanted to be part of it. They felt that space flight was the next step in the progress of aviation. The man who

(Left to right) Astronauts Carpenter, Cooper, Glenn, Grissom, Schirra, Shepard and Slayton—the first seven to be trained as American spacemen.

said, "There aren't many new frontiers. This is a chance to be in on one of them," spoke for the whole group.

These, then, were the men from whom the seven Mercury astronauts were to be chosen. Their test results were studied and studied again. Then the selection board looked at the past-performance record of each man and considered what special abilities he had that might prove valuable to Project Mercury.

Finally the choice was made—Malcolm Scott Carpenter, Leroy Gordon Cooper, Jr., John Herschel Glenn, Jr., Virgil Ivan Grissom, Walter Marty Schirra, Jr., Alan Bartlett Shepard, Jr., and Donald Kent Slayton.

VII. THE MERCURY ASTRONAUTS

Malcolm Scott Carpenter

One of the astronauts was beginning a tour of duty as an intelligence officer aboard the anti-submarine aircraft carrier *U.S.S. Hornet* when he was selected for Project Mercury. He was 33-year-old Navy Lieutenant Malcolm Scott Carpenter, who had just graduated from the Navy's Air Intelligence School in Washington, D.C.

Scott Carpenter's home town is Boulder, Colorado. After finishing high school there, he enrolled in the Navy's flight training program at Colorado College. He had progressed to primary flight training at Ottumwa, Iowa, when World War II ended. Carpenter returned to Colorado, where he studied aeronautical engineering at the state university. After graduating in 1949, he went back to the Navy and flight training. This time he won his wings of gold.

Following duty with Patrol Squadron 6 during the Korean conflict, Carpenter attended the Navy Test Pilot School. Then came several years of flight-testing Navy aircraft. He worked with the new jet fighters, the A-3D Skywarrior, the F-11F Tiger, and the F-9F Cougar. His assignment to the Naval Air Intelligence School followed, and then Project Mercury.

Most of Carpenter's flying had been in multi-engine planes. When he was selected for Project Mercury he had 2,800 hours of flying time, but only 300 hours of this was spent in jets—the least of any of the astronauts.

Carpenter was the second American astronaut to complete an orbital flight around the world. When Project Mercury ended he became a Project Gemini astronaut, but he made no more space flights. In 1967 Carpenter resigned from the space program to do deep-sea research for the Navy.

Leroy Gordon Cooper

The youngest of the astronauts also was the one to fly a plane at the youngest age. Leroy Gordon Cooper was only eight when he took over the controls for the first time. At 16 he had made his first solo flight. Flying was in his blood. His father was an Air Force officer and pilot, and young Leroy grew up with flyers and airplanes.

He was born March 6, 1927, in Shawnee, Oklahoma, and went to grade and high school there. When he graduated from high school in 1945, Leroy joined the Marine Corps. After his discharge a year later, he resumed his education at the University of Hawaii.

In 1949 Leroy Cooper was back in uniform. He had received a reserve officer's commission in the Army; this was transferred to the Air Force and the Air Force called him for flight training. After receiving his pilot's wings, Cooper went to Germany, where he flew the F-84 and F-86 jet fighters.

When he returned home, the Air Force sent him to school. He received a degree in aeronautical engineering from the Air Force Institute of Technology at Dayton, Ohio.

The Air Force Experimental Flight Test School came next and then an assignment testing experimental aircraft at Edwards Air Force Base in California. There he flew some of the Air Force's highest flying and fastest planes. In all he had some 2,300 hours of flying time—1,400 of it in jets. Cooper was a captain in the Air Force at the time of his selection.

On May 15–16, 1963, Astronaut Cooper's 22-orbit mission brought Project Mercury to a successful conclusion. He then transferred to Project Gemini and became the command pilot for the eight-day Gemini 5 flight. He later joined the Project Apollo space program.

John Herschel Glenn, Jr.

The oldest of the seven astronauts, and the first actually to orbit the earth, was green-eyed, red-haired John Herschel Glenn, Jr. He was 37 and a lieutenant colonel in the Marine Corps when selected for Project Mercury. John

Glenn grew up and went to high school in New Concord, Ohio, where his father operated a plumbing and heating business. When John graduated from high school in 1939, he became a student at New Concord's Muskingum College. He was a back on Muskingum's football team, the only one of the astronauts to engage in a major varsity sport.

The Japanese attack on Pearl Harbor brought a temporary halt to John Glenn's education. He enlisted in the naval aviation cadet program in March, 1942. He graduated a year later and chose to serve with the Marine Corps.

After the future astronaut won his wings in 1943, he was sent to the Marshall Islands in the Pacific as a member of Marine Fighter Squadron 155. He took part in 59 combat missions against the Japanese, flying the Corsair, one of the best fighter planes used in the Pacific theater.

When the war ended, John Glenn decided to remain in the Marine Corps. He had assignments in China, Guam, and the United States. During the Korean conflict he flew with both the Marines and the Air Force— a total of 90 combat missions during which he shot down three MIGs in nine days. He was awarded five Distinguished Flying Crosses and the Air Medal with 18 clusters for his service in World War II and in Korea.

After the Korean conflict was over, John Glenn became a test pilot. In his new job he worked with a number of advanced Navy aircraft. In one of them, the F-8U, he set a transcontinental speed record in 1957—

Left to right.
Malcolm Scott Carpenter
Leroy Gordon Cooper, Jr.
John Herschel Glenn, Jr.
Virgil Ivan Grissom
Walter Marty Schirra, Jr.
Alan Bartlett Shepard, Jr.
Donald Kent Slayton

Los Angeles to New York in 3 hours and 23 minutes. At the time he became a Mercury astronaut Glenn had more than 5,000 hours of flying time, 1,500 of it in jet aircraft.

Astronaut Glenn transferred to Project Gemini at the conclusion of the Mercury program. He retired in 1965, but continued to work with the National Aeronautics and Space Administration as a consultant.

Virgil Ivan Grissom

The second American astronaut to take a ride through space, Virgil Grissom, was from Mitchell, Indiana, where he was born in 1926. He started Air Force flight training as soon as he finished high school in 1944, but the war ended before he could finish. His short military career over, Grissom enrolled at Purdue University to study mechanical engineering. Four years later, when he graduated, he resumed his interrupted flight training. He won his wings in March, 1951, in time to fly a hundred combat missions in Korea in the F-86 Sabrejet fighter.

After Korea, Grissom became a flight instructor. In 1955 the Air Force sent him back to school for a year to study aeronautical engineering at its Institute of Technology located at Wright Patterson Air Force Base, Dayton, Ohio. Then he went to the test pilot school at Edwards Air Force Base. His assignment as a test pilot returned him to Wright Patterson, where he tested fighter planes. He had over 3,000 hours of flying time, more than 2,000 of it in jets.

Grissom, who was captain in the Air Force at the time of selection, almost didn't get to be an astronaut. He had chronic hay fever. When the doctors at the Lovelace Clinic were ready to disqualify him, Grissom successfully argued that there would be no ragweed pollen in space. And for good measure he would be sealed in a pressurized cabin. With his physical examinations safely behind him, he went on to do extremely well in the stress tests. The ability to stay calm in an emergency, which had made him a good test pilot, helped him to become an astronaut.

From Project Mercury, Grissom moved to Project Gemini. He flew a successful three-orbit Gemini mission on March 23, 1965. Astronaut Grissom, who had transferred to the Apollo program, was named command pilot of the first manned Apollo mission. While preparing for that flight he was killed in a flash fire aboard an Apollo spacecraft on January 27, 1967, during a simulated countdown.

Walter Marty Schirra, Jr.

When he was called to Washington to be interviewed for Project Mercury, Walter Marty Schirra, Jr., was working with one of the Navy's newest planes, the twin-jet McDonnell F-4H fighter. For a while he hesitated about volunteering for Project Mercury, because he felt that the Navy's jet development program was an important one, too. However, after thinking it over, he decided that he could make a greater contribution as an astronaut, and his answer was yes. He would volunteer for Project Mercury.

Schirra's interest in flying began at an early age. His father was a World War I flyer and, after the war, he became a barnstorming pilot who traveled around the eastern part of the United States giving flying exhibitions in a light plane.

Walter Schirra, Jr. was born March 12, 1923, in Hackensack, New Jersey. After attending grade and high school and one year of engineering college in New Jersey, he won an appointment to the United States Naval Academy.

After his graduation in 1945, Schirra served at sea for a few years before he applied for flight training. He won his wings at Pensacola, Florida, and became a Navy fighter pilot.

When the Korean conflict broke out, Schirra was an exchange pilot with the Air Force's 154th Fighter Bomber Squadron. His 90 combat missions in Korea were with this squadron. Flying a F-84 jet fighter, he downed one MIG and possibly another.

Back again with the Navy, Schirra worked with the Sidewinder missile and the Navy's new F-7U3 Cutlass and F-J3 Fury jet fighters before entering test-pilot training. When he became an astronaut, 1,700 of his 3,000 flying hours were in jets. He was a lieutenant commander in the Navy at the time of his selection.

Astronaut Schirra made a six-orbit Mercury flight in 1962. In 1965 he was at the controls of Gemini 6 when it successfully rendezvoused in space with Gemini 7. Schirra subsequently transferred to the Project Apollo program and in 1968 was the command pilot of the first manned Apollo mission.

Alan Bartlett Shepard

America's first spaceman, Astronaut Alan Bartlett Shepard, was a Navy man like Schirra. Before his selection for Project Mercury, he was a lieutenant commander serving as an aircraft readiness officer on the staff of the commander of the Atlantic Fleet.

Astronaut Shepard was born November 18, 1923, in East Derry, New Hampshire. He went to school there and spent a year at the Admiral Farragut Academy in Toms River, New Jersey, before entering the United States Naval Academy.

After his graduation from Annapolis in 1944, Shepard spent the last year of the war on the destroyer *Cogswell* in the Pacific. He then entered flight training, receiving his pilot's wings in March, 1947. Following duty in this country and in the Mediterranean as a fighter pilot, Shepard was sent to test-pilot school. As a test pilot he took part in high-altitude flights to study light at different levels and in different air masses. He also helped with the development of the Navy's in-flight re-

fueling system and tested some of the Navy's new jet
fighters. Almost half of his 3,600 hours of flying time
had been in jets.

At the conclusion of the Project Mercury program
Shepard joined Project Gemini. When an inner-ear injury
made it impossible for him to make any more space flights,
he became NASA's chief astronaut, an administrative
position.

Donald Kent Slayton

Donald Kent Slayton served with the Air Force in both
combat theaters during World War II. He flew 56 combat missions as a B-25 pilot in Europe and, after a short
period back home as an instructor, flew seven missions
over Japan.

The future astronaut was born on March 1, 1924, in
Sparta, Wisconsin, and graduated from high school
there in 1942. He entered the Air Force as an aviation
cadet and won his wings a year later.

After the war Slayton enrolled at the University of
Minnesota to study aeronautical engineering. He got
his degree in 1949 and went to work for the Boeing Aircraft Company in Seattle, Washington. When he was
called back to active duty by the Air Force in 1951,
Slayton decided to make the Air Force his career.

He was serving as a fighter pilot in Germany when
he was assigned to the Air Force Flight Test Pilot
School at Edwards Air Force Base. He stayed on at
Edwards to become an experimental test pilot special-

izing in jet fighters. Of his 3,400 hours in the air, 2,000 were in jets. He was an Air Force captain when selected to be an astronaut.

Slayton made no space flights as a Mercury astronaut. In 1962 an Air Force medical team ruled that a minor heart palpitation could bar him from further military flying. Shortly thereafter he resigned from the Air Force to become NASA's director of flight-crew operations.

VIII. THE MERCURY ASTRONAUTS GET READY TO EXPLORE SPACE

"Gentlemen, these are the astronaut volunteers."

The speaker was Walter Bonney, the National Aeronautics and Space Administration's press chief. The place was NASA's Washington headquarters. The time was two o'clock on the afternoon of April 9, 1959. The final selection of the Mercury astronauts had been made a few days earlier; now they were being presented to the public for the first time.

Behind Mr. Bonney as he made his announcement sat Donald K. Slayton, Alan B. Shepard, Jr., Walter M. Schirra, Jr., Virgil I. Grissom, John H. Glenn, Jr., Leroy G. Cooper, Jr., and Malcolm S. Carpenter, seven poised young men in business suits. They were about to embark on an intensive period of training for manned space flight. One of them would be the first American to travel in space. All of them would play a big part in making Project Mercury a success.

A training headquarters for the astronauts had already been set up at Langley Field, an Air Force base in southern Virginia. Langley would be "home" to the astronauts, but they would spend considerable time in other places, working with the manufacturers of space equipment and using training devices not available at Langley. Carrying orders from the Air Force, the Navy, or the Marine Corps—orders which assigned them for duty with NASA on a full-time basis—the seven Project Mercury astronauts arrived at Langley to begin the most challenging job of their careers. Not only would they be learning to fly an entirely new type of craft, they would also be helping to develop both the craft and the techniques for its operation.

Training at Langley began with a series of briefings in which members of the Space Task Group explained Project Mercury in detail. Each of the seven astronauts was assigned an area in which to specialize. Carpenter's was communications and navigational aids; Cooper was given the Redstone rocket to be used in suborbital shots. To Glenn went the job of helping to plan the space capsule's cockpit. The various automatic and manual devices for controlling the flight of the capsule were to be Grissom's specialty; Schirra's was the capsule's life-support system. Shepard was assigned to work with the plans for tracking and recovering the capsule, and to Slayton went the mighty Atlas booster that would lift the capsule into orbit.

A part of the astronauts' time at Langley was spent in "school." Because of the many demands that would be made on them during their training and during their rides through space, it was important that they have a good working knowledge of the basic sciences. Astronomy, physics, geography, and meteorology were given to them in big doses. Experts lectured on such subjects as aviation biology, ballistics, the principles of propulsion, and gyroscopic theory. For "home work" they were given technical reports to study. Along with a thorough understanding of the mechanics of space travel, they were acquiring the knowledge they would need to make detailed observations of themselves and their surroundings while in space.

Not all of the astronauts' time was spent in the classroom. They learned a great deal about space flight by actually going through the procedures they would someday use. They couldn't practice space flight in space, of course, but they did the next best thing. They used devices cleverly constructed to reproduce the conditions of space flight. These machines, called simulators, were first developed to help train airplane pilots, and they had become almost uncanny in the way they could make a man think he was actually flying an airplane.

Developing simulators for space flight was a more difficult process. Until the first space flight had actually been completed, there was no way of knowing for sure just what conditions should be reproduced. One of the most complicated of the simulators developed at Langley was one to produce the effect of orbital flight motion. An astronaut's couch was suspended in midair before a circular motion picture screen. Reclining on this couch as he would during a space flight, the astronaut, through a periscope, watched films as they were

At Langley Field John Glenn practices space-craft instrument procedures in a training device that resembles a Mercury capsule.

projected on the screen. The films, taken by a missile, showed the earth as it looks from 100 miles up in space. As he watched, the astronaut "flew" his capsule. He made corrections with his control stick in accordance with the picture he got of the earth. The couch floated on an air jet. Smaller jets, controlled by the astronaut's stick, changed its attitude or direction. After hours of practice in this simulator, the astronaut wouldn't be afraid to maneuver his capsule if he wanted to get a better look at something while in space. And in the unlikely event that his instruments should fail, he would know that he could navigate by using his periscope to look at the earth below him.

Another simulator was developed to give the astronaut practice in maneuvering the space capsule during its turbulent reëntry into the earth's atmosphere. In this one the astronaut was placed in front of an instrument panel equipped with dials to indicate how straight and level his capsule was "flying." When the dials indicated a condition that needed correction—too much rolling motion, for example—he would have to correct it by using his control stick.

For some of their training the astronauts had to travel to Johnsville, Pennsylvania. There at the Navy's Acceleration Laboratory, they rode in a giant centrifuge which duplicated the acceleration and deceleration stresses the astronaut would have to endure during his space flight. Acceleration occurs when a moving object gains speed. If you have ridden in a jet airplane, you must have felt the effects of acceleration when the plane took off and

Top. *An astronaut steps into the gondola suspended from the 50-foot arm of the Johnsville centrifuge.* Bottom. *His face contorted by acceleration stresses, Scott Carpenter struggles to work his control stick in the whirling centrifuge.*

your body was forced back against the seat. Deceleration occurs when a moving object loses speed. When you ride in a car that comes to a sudden stop, you feel the effects of deceleration.

In the course of his trip through space, the astronaut would experience rapid acceleration on take-off and rapid deceleration on reëntry into the earth's atmosphere. If the booster rocket failed and the escape rocket went into action, there would be violent acceleration as the capsule shot away, followed by deceleration as it slowed against the atmosphere.

The stresses the human body experiences during acceleration or deceleration are expressed in terms of g-numbers. Gravity pulls everyone to the earth with a force of one g. Since this pull is always present, we never notice it. However, if it were to be doubled we would experience difficulty in walking or climbing. At three g's we wouldn't be able to walk or climb at all. At four g's we could barely crawl, and five g's would make it difficult to move even an arm. For each of these g's we would be feeling a pull equal to the total number of g's multiplied by our weight. If we weighed 100 pounds, at 5 g's we would experience a pull, or force, of 500 pounds. No wonder we would be unable to move!

The centrifuge at Johnsville gave the astronauts valuable experience under the stress of as many as 20 g's. It also developed their ability to withstand the effects of rapid acceleration or deceleration because they found that, with practice, they could perform as well at 16 g's as they did during their first rides at 10 g's.

The Johnsville centrifuge was a pill-shaped gondola suspended at the end of a 50-foot arm. A 180-ton motor whirled the arm around at tremendous speeds. The gondola could be rotated to produce the effect of acceleration on take-off or deceleration on reëntry. Strapped to a supporting couch, the astronaut rode the ten-by-six-foot gondola. He wore his helmet and, for the more strenuous rides, his pressure suit.

When the centrifuge began to whirl, the g's increased rapidly, as they would during an actual space flight. As they mounted, the astronaut's heart rate and respiration were recorded. After the ride there were further checks to determine if the high g's had injured him in any way.

The gondola had the same instruments and controls as the Mercury capsule. During his ride the astronaut tried to do the things he would do if he were "flying" his capsule—speak into his microphone, read his instruments, manipulate his control stick—in spite of the stress of the high g forces. When the ride is all over and he gets out of the gondola, the astronaut is exhausted. His muscles are sore and he feels bruised, but he knows that he has successfully "flown" under the stress of higher g forces than he is likely to encounter in an actual space flight.

Another training device was located at NASA's Lewis Research Center in Cleveland. This was the Multiple

Axis Space Test Facility, or MASTIF, a machine developed to give the astronauts practice in controlling the capsule when it shot free of the burned-out booster rocket. An automatic control system would normally steady the capsule, but if it failed the astronaut would have to do the controlling himself.

MASTIF had three metal frameworks surrounding a chair in which the pilot sat. Each one of the three produced a different kind of tumbling motion. The rider could be spun in only one direction or he could be spun in three directions at once. The astronauts found spinning in one direction no problem, but spinning in three directions at the same time was something else again! They had to fight to focus their eyes on the control dial, to force themselves to read it, and then make the movements with the control stick that would gradually bring the spinning MASTIF to a halt. They emerged weak and wobbly from their ordeal but confident that, no matter how much their Mercury capsule tumbled about in space, they would be able to control it.

To prepare for the sensation of weightlessness they would encounter in space, the astronauts took a series of airplane rides in which they were weightless for periods as long as a minute. During orbital flights they would be weightless for several hours, but there was no way to keep them weightless that long without sending them up into space. Three kinds of planes were used, the Air Force C-131, C-135 and F-100F.

During the rides in the two-seater F-100F, the jet plane climbed to 40,000 feet. Then with the after-

Astronaut Grissom sits in the MASTIF chair, surrounded by three metal frameworks which can spin him in three directions at once.

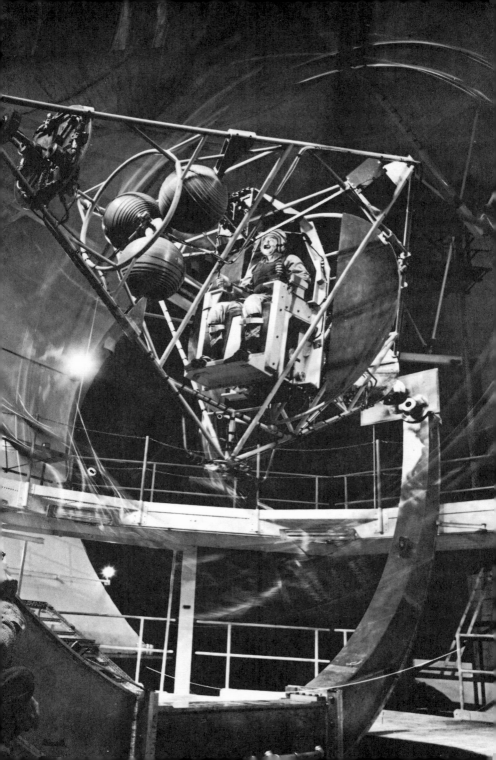

burner on to give more power, down it went in a fast 30-degree dive to 25,000 feet. Then up it streaked again at full power until it reached the point where the climbing momentum of the plane canceled out the pull of gravity. For 60 seconds the plane and its occupants were weightless. During this time the astronaut had various tasks to perform. On some of his rides he practiced eating from squeeze bottles; on others he took short tests to see how well he could perform while weightless. When he got back on the ground there were more tests to see if he had suffered any ill effects from the short period of weightlessness. No problems at all developed during the rides, but there was no way of telling for sure what the result would be when the weightlessness lasted for four hours or more.

Another part of the Mercury flight—getting out of the capsule after it made its water landing—called for considerable practice beforehand. In a pool at Langley and later in the Gulf of Mexico, in calm water and in high waves, the seven astronauts got themselves out of a floating capsule. They had to release the straps holding them to their couch, unfasten the various hoses and wires running from their pressure suits, and remove part of the instrument panel to get to the escape hatch at the top of the capsule. Life raft and survival kit went through the hatch first, followed by the astronaut who then tied his inflated raft to the capsule to await rescue. A great deal of salt water was swallowed in these maneuvers, but the astronauts learned they could leave the capsule through the top hatch if they had to.

Three astronauts experience weightlessness during a zero gravity ride in a C-131 airplane.

The busy astronauts had still other forms of training. They spent hours in pressure chambers, in dark sound-proof rooms, and in steam rooms. And they did enough flying in the F-102 jet fighter to keep up their proficiency as pilots. The Mercury astronauts were going to be ready for that first trip into space.

IX. TEST SHOTS FOR
PROJECT MERCURY

While the seven astronauts were spinning madly in the MASTIF or whirling around in the centrifuge, the Mercury capsule was undergoing tests, too. Through a series of trial shots it was moving closer and closer to the goal of Project Mercury—manned orbital flight. A special solid-fuel launch vehicle was developed to lift some of the early test capsules. Called Little Joe, it had a launch thrust of 250,000 pounds, enough to reach a fairly high altitude. Beginning in the fall of 1959, several Little Joes were used in tests designed primarily to check the operation of the capsule's escape system under various emergency conditions. Before an astronaut could be shot into space, the escape system had to be foolproof.

Most of the capsules launched with the Little Joes were development, or boilerplate, models. Next came tests with production-type capsules—the real thing—and with more powerful launch vehicles, the Redstone and Atlas boosters. The Redstone was the in-between booster. More powerful than the Little Joe, it still lacked the necessary thrust to put a capsule into orbit. The Atlas could do that. The Redstone was used to test Mercury capsules on short-range, ballistic flights up into space and back down again.

The first attempt to launch a capsule with a Redstone booster got nowhere at all. The Redstone rose about four inches and then settled back, acquiring some dents in the process. It had to be replaced. A month later, on December 19, 1960, the first Mercury-Redstone flight took off for space. It was a success although the capsule came down a little too fast.

The necessary adjustments were made, and the Mercury-Redstone combination was tried again. At Cape Canaveral, on January 31, 1961, a capsule was launched carrying a three-year-old chimpanzee named Ham. After a breakfast of baby cereal, condensed milk, half an egg, cooking oil and gelatin, Ham had been strapped to a specially designed contour couch. His arms were free because he had work to do. Above his couch was a system of lights and levers which Ham had been trained to use. A white light flashed when he pulled the correct lever, and he got a mild shock unless he pulled it every 20 seconds. To complicate things, a blue light flashed every two minutes warning him of an impending shock unless he pulled still another lever.

Ham was able to manipulate his levers successfully in spite of 6½ minutes of weightlessness and the force of 14.6 g's he encountered on the way back down. His trip in space lasted 18 minutes. However, a malfunction in the booster caused Ham to travel 421 miles—116

Top. *The first Mercury capsule successfully launched by a Redstone booster is lowered onto the deck of the USS Valley Forge.* Bottom. *Ham, the first chimpanzee sent into space, reaches out for an apple after his ride.*

miles farther than had been planned. Consequently he overshot the recovery ships. To add to his troubles, his capsule keeled over and took on some water after it had been in the ocean awhile. A helicopter arrived before much damage was done, but a worried Ham emerged from the capsule after it had been lifted to the deck of the recovery ship. He was given an immediate checkup. The trip had not harmed him in any way, and after he had eaten an apple he felt much better.

The 37-pound Ham was the heaviest passenger the Mercury capsule had carried, but he wasn't the first. Two of the Little Joe rockets had lifted capsules carrying passengers, the rhesus monkeys Sam and Miss Sam. Both were safely recovered from the Atlantic after successful operation of the capsule escape system, an achievement that pleased Project Mercury officials and, no doubt, Sam and Miss Sam as well.

The Redstone flight that followed Ham's trip into space carried no passenger. His misadventures had indicated that some corrections would have to be made in both the booster and the capsule. This new flight was to insure that everything was now in good working order. It was, so Project Mercury could take another big step forward. A Redstone was used to lift a man into space. The man was Astronaut Alan Shepard and, as we have already seen, his space trip was an extremely successful step forward. The Redstone worked perfectly, and all the capsule's complicated systems performed in a satisfactory manner.

May 5, 1961, was a happy day for Project Mercury, but Shepard's one flight wasn't enough to insure that the capsule was absolutely reliable. A second manned flight would provide a better test. Preparations were made to send up one more Redstone-boosted capsule to duplicate Freedom 7's successful trip. There would be some changes. The next capsule would have a "picture" window and the astronaut would have more time to look around and observe his space environment.

Which one of the astronauts would go this time? It proved to be Virgil Grissom, one of the three men alerted for the Redstone flights. He had helped with the preparations for the May 5 flight. And two months later, on July 21, 1961, he was the man that climbed into the capsule for the second trial.

His trip started off smoothly enough. In fact it was smoother than Astronaut Shepard's, for the capsule had been modified to cut down the vibration that gave Shepard such a shaking at 36,000 feet. Grissom commented later: "This is one problem I feel we have licked."

He described the new window as "about like a keyhole to me, but it is a big window, anyway for a space flight." He began to look through it almost at once, watching the blue sky of the launching change to a pitch black as he gained altitude. And right in the center of the window he saw a star. That star cost the astronaut two steak dinners. He had bet John Glenn that they would not be able to see stars in flight. Shepard had seen none on his flight.

Like Shepard, Astronaut Grissom heard with considerable relief the sound of the escape rocket firing when the Redstone's engine cut off. Then he saw the escape tower shoot off to the right. The capsule's parachutes are located underneath the escape system. If the escape rocket doesn't fire, the parachutes can't be used. This would result in a hard landing. In describing the sound the escape rocket made as it fired, Grissom said: "It was really comforting."

There was a bright sun shining in the black sky—so bright, in fact, that at one point the astronaut was afraid he might be blinded by the light. The shaft of sunlight didn't reach his face, however, and he was able to go through the same procedures for controlling the motion of the capsule that Shepard had used.

The new window proved to be almost too much of an attraction. Grissom reported that he was so fascinated by what he could see—the horizon, the clouds, and the sky shading from a light blue to a deep black—that he had difficulty concentrating on his control maneuvers.

Soon it was time to fire the retro-rockets to slow the capsule. Grissom did this manually. Then he started down. He had a smooth descent. The g forces reached 10.2 as the capsule entered the earth's atmosphere—not enough, though, to cause him any difficulty. His parachutes came out on schedule; his landing was "a pretty good bump, but nothing that would jar me."

So far it was a very successful flight, but there was still time for things to go wrong. And they did.

The capsule fell over on its left side when it hit, but

Top. *Virgil Grissom (left) and his alternate, John Glenn, eat an early morning breakfast before Grissom's flight.* Bottom. *In the Mercury Control Center astronauts Glenn, Schirra and Shepard intently follow Grissom's launch.*

it soon righted itself. Grissom began recording the positions of his switches and gauges for later study at Cape Canaveral. He had already partially prepared himself for leaving the capsule—unfastened his straps, loosened his helmet, and disconnected most of the wires and lines running from his suit. Helicopters were standing by. When the astronaut was ready to be picked up, he notified them. While he waited, he removed the cover of the detonator that would blow the side hatch open, and pulled the safety pin. And then it happened. The hatch blew off! As Grissom described it later: "I was lying there, all in business, and pow, the hatch blew up and I looked up and saw nothing but blue sky and water started to come in over the sill."

One look was enough for him. He tossed off his helmet and got out. The helicopter pilot reported that Grissom followed immediately behind the door. It was almost one motion. The helicopter darted down toward the capsule hoping to get a line on it before it sank. Grissom, held up by his space suit, tried to help, but the wash from the helicopter's rotors blew him away.

The first helicopter on the scene had been joined by three others, but there was no saving the Liberty Bell 7, as Grissom's capsule had been named. The five-million-dollar, instrument-laden Liberty Bell 7 was full of water and too heavy to lift. Astronaut Grissom was in trouble, too. Water was coming in through an opening in his suit and he was beginning to sink. He was surrounded by helicopters but he couldn't get to any of them. Finally one of the chopper pilots got in close

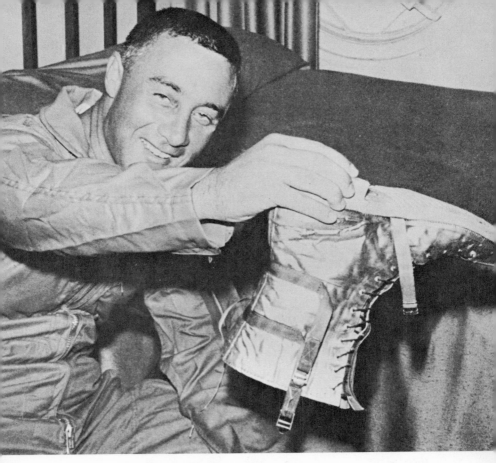

Aboard the USS Randolph, Grissom jokingly empties the sea water from his boot after taking off his space suit.

enough to lower a sling. Grissom was picked up and taken to the waiting recovery ship *Randolph.*

Later when a reporter asked him if he had been frightened at any time during his space flight, Grissom replied with a grin: "I was scared." When he was asked whether space flight was as interesting as Astronaut Shepard had reported it to be, Grissom said: "It certainly was; I'd recommend the trip to anyone."

Astronaut Grissom had traveled 307 miles from Cape Canaveral. He had reached a height of 118 miles, and he had been weightless for five minutes. His was the last Mercury flight to use the Redstone rocket. The malfunctioning hatch door would have to be studied, but there were no more test objectives that could be achieved with the Redstone. The next step was orbital flight with the more powerful Atlas.

An attempt to place a Mercury capsule in orbit with the Atlas had failed on April 25, 1961. The rocket's steering mechanism had not worked properly. It was September before the Atlas finally lifted the capsule into orbit for one trip around the earth. It was a regulation capsule, but there was no life aboard.

It was extremely desirable that the capsule be given a longer test, at least three times around the earth, and that its life support system be tested on something alive. In spite of a growing public interest in getting a man into orbit before the end of 1961, Project Mercury officials went ahead with their plans to attempt an orbital shot with a chimpanzee as a passenger before they sent up an astronaut. So instead of one of the astronauts it was Enos, the astrochimp, who prepared for the next Mercury flight.

Enos was a 37-pound chimp, about the size of a husky four-year-old boy, who had been trained for space flight at a special school at Holloman Air Force Base in New Mexico. He was shot up into orbit on the morning of November 29, 1961. Like the chimpanzee Ham before him, Enos had work to do while he was in space—levers to push in response to a set of signals. His lever-pushing was monitored electronically by scientists on the ground, who were interested in finding out whether prolonged weightlessness would affect his performance.

The astrochimp seemed to be doing all right, but during his second sweep around the earth, things started to go wrong with the capsule. A set of inverters began heating up and so did Enos' cabin. The mechanism for controlling the movement of the capsule was using up the hydrogen-peroxide fuel supply at a rapid rate. The capsule was brought down after it had completed only two orbits.

That complicated maneuver went off without a hitch; the capsule, with Enos inside, was plucked out of the Atlantic south of Bermuda. Enos appeared to have survived his 180-minute trip in fine style. Later, a detailed study of the records revealed that his blood pressure had gone up at the start of the journey and stayed up until he got out of the capsule. Poor Enos had reasons for being upset. He was supposed to get a slight shock when he pushed the incorrect levers. Something went wrong and he was getting a shock even when he pushed the right ones. The trouble with the hydrogen-peroxide fuel-supply system had caused the capsule to rock and Enos had rocked right along with it.

But Enos' difficulties were only temporary. In general, the flight was considered to be a success. So the next Mercury capsule shot into orbit could carry one of the astronauts!

X. OTHER UNITED STATES SPACE PROJECTS

Although Mercury was a high-priority project, it was not the National Aeronautics and Space Administration's only assault on space. Airplanes powered by rockets had been under consideration for high-altitude research before Project Mercury was born. And the X-15 rocket plane was undergoing tests at the same time as the Mercury capsule. Jointly sponsored by NASA and the Air Force, the X-15 program was designed to obtain information on the problems of manned flight at extremely high altitudes.

Headquarters for work with the X-15 was Edwards Air Force Base, located in southern California's Mojave Desert. A 65-square-mile dry lake bed near the base served as a landing field for the rocket plane. The X-15 landed on skids instead of wheels.

There were other things that were different about the X-15. For wings it had a stubby wedge sticking out from each side of the fuselage. Its tail was a huge vertical fin; its nose was a sharp needle. All of its 50-foot length was covered with a dull black, heat-resistant paint. Its skin was made of Inconel-X, a nickel alloy that can take temperatures up to 1,200 degrees Fahrenheit. Its interior was divided into a small pilot's cockpit, two huge tanks for liquid oxygen and ammonia and, in the rear, a powerful rocket engine. The X-15 was something new, half-airplane and half-missile. It was a missile that could fly back from space.

The X-15 took off tucked under the wing of an eight-jet B-52. The pilot, wearing a full pressure suit, was already in the X-15's narrow cockpit. He was strapped to an ejection seat and surrounded by switches, buttons, and gauges. Three control sticks were within easy reach. All along the route that the rocket plane would follow as it flew back to Edwards, technicians were waiting with sensitive tracking and monitoring equipment. The X-15 was loaded with instruments to measure, record, and report everything that happened to plane and pilot. This was a research plane. It flew only so that the effects of high altitude and high speed could be studied.

The B-52 jet carried the 16½-ton X-15 nearly 500 miles, climbing until it could climb no higher. Then it turned to point the X-15 toward Edwards. By this time they were at an altitude of 40,000 feet over Wendover Air Force Base near Salt Lake City, Utah. The flight track of the X-15 ran from Wendover back to Edwards Air Force Base.

The X-15 pilot had been working on his pre-launch check list. He now began the final checks, keeping in touch with the B-52 mother ship by radio. If all of the numerous and complicated systems were working prop-

An X-15 rocket plane tucked under the wing of a B-52.

erly, he notified the B-52 that he was ready for the launch
to send him flying off on his own.

The needle-nosed X-15 dropped like a rock from under
the mother ship's wing, but its rocket engine took over
at once, shooting it skyward. Within seconds the B-52 was
far behind and below. As he climbed, the X-15 pilot experienced the same acceleration forces that hit the Mercury astronauts on their take-offs. He too had trained for
them in the centrifuge at Johnsville. He could adjust his
control sticks with the touch of a finger, and a finger was
about all he could move at that point.

He climbed higher and higher, aiming for an altitude 50
miles above the earth. At 40 miles, the X-15's engine, having exhausted its fuel supply, cut out, but the ship continued to climb. It was carried forward now by the momentum of its great speed, higher and still higher. But
acceleration was beginning to fall off. The pilot was no
longer squashed back into his seat. The force pushing
against him became less and less and finally disappeared
altogether. Now he was weightless.

The X-15, being both spaceship and plane, had two
sets of controls—one for use at lower levels and one
for use at altitudes where there was not enough atmosphere to support a plane's control surfaces. To maneuver
his craft as he floated 50 miles above the earth, the pilot
used the control stick at his left. It activated hydrogen-
peroxide jets in the nose and wing tips, a steering process somewhat similar to that used in the Mercury capsule.

Under its own power the X-15 takes off from the mother ship.

When the X-15 had exhausted its climbing momentum and started back down to earth, it traveled at a tremendous speed. The plane was built to go faster than 4,000 miles an hour. As it pushed through the thickening atmosphere, its metal skin began to heat up. A metal other than Inconel-X would have melted. Air conditioning in the cockpit and in his suit kept the pilot cool.

Down where the air was thicker, the pilot abandoned the left control stick and began to use the ones on his right and in the center. These were aerodynamic controls similar to those found on more conventional planes, and with them he guided the X-15 back to the dry lake bed at Edwards.

Three teams of test pilots worked with the X-15 project. North American Aviation, its manufacturer, had two test pilots assigned to the experimental plane. They were Scott Crossfield, the chief engineering pilot, and Alvin White, his back-up. They were responsible for thoroughly testing each of the X-15s to make sure it was airworthy and capable of meeting performance standards.

After North American finished its test program, two other teams took over. One made research flights for the National Aeronautics and Space Administration and the other made flights for the Air Force. The men who made up the teams were all experienced test pilots especially selected and trained to fly the three experimental X-15 rocket planes.

Before he flew a mission, an X-15 test pilot spent many hours drawing up precise plans for his flight. He spent another 50 hours or so in an X-15 simulator practicing the procedures he would use during his ten minutes of actual flying. And it took at least two hours to check the experimental plane and its systems before each flight.

The first flights of the X-15 were glide tests. It was dropped from the B-52 mother ship to glide back to Edwards Air Force Base without using its rocket engine. The first powered flight of the X-15 took place on September 17, 1959, with Scott Crossfield at the controls. He reached a speed of 1,385 miles an hour on that first flight.

That was just the beginning. Plans for the X-15 called for a gradual increase in speed until 4,000 miles an hour was reached and a gradual increase in altitude to 250,000 feet. Within a few years both of these goals had been reached and the rocket plane went on to surpass them. In 1963 the X-15 climbed to an altitude record of 354,200 feet, more than 67 miles. Eight pilots have flown the X-15 higher than 50 miles. The five who were military pilots were awarded astronauts' wings by the Air Force.

In 1967 the X-15 flew a record-breaking 4,520 miles an hour, more than seven times the speed of sound.

The X-15 program was not without its mishaps. Its rocket engine exploded both in the air and during run-up on the ground. Temperature changes of more than 1,000 degrees in less than three minutes splintered its windshield during flight. Each of the three X-15s had to be rebuilt or modified as problem areas developed. And in 1967 one of them was completely destroyed in a crash.

From the X-15 program NASA and the Air Force gained much valuable information about how pilot and plane function at high speeds and high altitudes. The special

Top. An X-15 pilot guides the craft to a landing on the dry lake bed at Edwards Air Force Base. Bottom. Joseph Walker, Robert White and Scott Crossfield, three X-15 test pilots, confer beside one of the rocket ships.

metal-working techniques developed for the X-15's Inconel skin have been used in other aircraft. The X-15's sensitive guidance and control systems have been adapted for use in both aircraft and rockets. In addition, the X-15 has participated in scientific experiments involving such activities as measuring the sun's radiation and gathering dust and micrometeoroids from the edge of space.

While some of NASA's scientists and technicians worked on manned high-altitude and space projects, others were developing better methods of unmanned space exploration. One of the first of these unmanned research programs was called Explorer. NASA acquired Explorer from the Army in 1958 after Explorer space craft had already begun investigating the radiation belts. Since then Explorer has become a multi-purpose satellite program. Each of the several Explorers sent into orbit every year is designed to carry out a specific set of experiments. Although Explorers are relatively small satellites, they have returned much valuable data to earth.

NASA's Pioneer research program began investigating radiation in space in 1958. The first three Pioneer space-craft returned some information, but they failed to achieve the desired flight path. Pioneer 4, however, went into orbit around the sun, the first American satellite to do so. Other Pioneers have also been sent into a solar orbit to study magnetic fields, cosmic dust and other phenomena of the interplanetary regions.

While the Pioneer program was underway, NASA developed still another unmanned space craft to study the sun and its influence upon the earth. The first Orbiting Solar

Observatory (OSO) was successfully launched in 1962. It was followed by several others which have sent back information on such things as solar flares and radiation.

Unlike an ordinary space craft, an orbiting observatory provides a stable platform for the delicate instruments that it carries, many of them supplied by the country's observatories and scientific laboratories. The OSO was one of three orbiting observatories developed by NASA to obtain more information about the universe. The Orbiting Astronomical Observatory (OAO) was designed to provide a stable platform for a thousand pounds of telescopes, radiation detecting devices and other equipment. The OAO travels in an orbit approximately 500 miles from the surface of the earth, well above the obscuring effects of the atmosphere.

NASA's Orbiting Geophysical Observatory (OGO) can carry from 20 to 30 experiments on a single mission. One of the space agency's most complex unmanned satellites, OGO was developed to supply information on such phenomena of the interplanetary environment as solar wind, solar flares, cosmic rays, magnetic fields and micrometeoroids. NASA places its OGOs in a variety of earth orbits, depending on the subjects to be studied.

Another family of unmanned space craft has helped explore the moon. The first of these, called Ranger, took photographs before making a "hard," or crash, landing on the moon. Between 1961 and 1965, when the program ended, Rangers sent back over 17,000 photographs of the lunar surface.

Surveyors were the next space craft to go to the moon.

Because they used braking rockets to make a "soft" landing, Surveyors were able to carry instruments as well as cameras. Since the program began in 1966, Surveyors have sent back high-quality photographs of the lunar surface and valuable reports on the composition of lunar soil.

The last of the unmanned moon-exploring space craft, called Lunar Orbiter, traveled around the moon to gather information about possible landing sites for Project Apollo, NASA's program for a manned expedition to the moon. Lunar Orbiters have transmitted both photographs and scientific data.

One of NASA's unmanned space craft was designed to send information to earth as it flew past Venus or Mars. Mariner 1, launched in 1962, had to be destroyed, but later that year Mariner 2 flew past Venus and established a long-distance communications record. Other Mariners have also successfully flown past Venus and some have flown past Mars.

Along with NASA's manned space programs, its unmanned investigations have added to our knowledge of the universe. And information obtained from the unmanned space craft has helped NASA prepare for its manned space shots.

XI. THE SOVIET UNION'S SPACE PIONEERS

"The Soviet Union has successfully launched a manned spaceship-satellite into orbit around the earth. Present aboard the spaceship is the pilot cosmonaut, Yuri Gagarin, an air force pilot, 27 years of age!"

This radio announcement, made in Moscow on the morning of April 12, 1961, was greeted with great joy by the Russian people. And as the news of Cosmonaut Gagarin's feat spread, congratulations poured into Moscow from countries all over the world.

President John F. Kennedy, in his congratulatory message, said: "The achievement of the U.S.S.R. of orbiting a man and returning him to the ground is an outstanding technical accomplishment. We congratulate the Soviet scientists and engineers who made this feat possible. The exploration of our solar system is an ambition which we and all mankind share with the Soviet Union and this is an important step toward that goal. Our own Mercury man-in-space program is directed toward the same end."

Indeed it was an important step forward in space exploration. For the first time man had succeeded in freeing himself from the forces that confined him to the planet Earth. He had traveled in space and returned safely, a truly great accomplishment.

Many years of research and experimentation had preceded the successful space flight. Because the Soviet Union releases very little information about its scientific programs, the world may never know all the developments that led up to Cosmonaut Gagarin's flight, but certainly the very best Soviet scientists and engineers worked hard to bring it about.

We have already seen how, in 1957, the Soviet Union had been the first country to successfully launch an unmanned earth satellite and the first to launch a satellite carrying a passenger. That passenger was the dog Laika, who did not survive the trip. The next year two dogs were sent up into space in a special pressurized capsule. They did not travel around the earth, but came down safely after reaching a height of 280 miles. Soon the Soviet Union had several dogs who were veterans of space trips; some of them had been up more than once. The dogs were studied carefully during their journeys. Soviet scientists were gathering information to help them send a man into space.

They were also building and launching spaceships of the type used for Yuri Gagarin's trip. Five of them were sent aloft in the year preceding his successful orbiting of the earth. These spaceships were considerably larger and heavier than the Project Mercury capsules. They weighed over five tons! The powerful boosters developed by Soviet rocket experts could lift a great deal more than the American Atlas.

The Soviet spaceships were described as having two sections. One section was for instruments and the braking mechanism, and the other was a fairly spacious cabin for the pilot, who rode in an ejection seat. By pressing a button he could eject himself and his seat from the cabin. The seat contained the equipment he would need for a forced landing—food, water, radio, a portable oxygen supply, and flares and other devices to attract rescuers.

Inside the cabin the temperature was maintained between 50 and 71.6 degrees Fahrenheit. Air pressure and humidity were regulated at a comfortable level. As in the Mercury capsule, many of the systems were duplicated to insure the cosmonaut's health and safety. Enough supplies were carried to last for ten days.

From his seat the cosmonaut could see the instrument panel with its rotating globe to show him where he was. He could reach the control panel, the flight-control stick, an electric clock, and a radio. His cabin had portholes through which he could look during flight.

The spaceship in which Cosmonaut Gagarin traveled was called the *Vostok,* or East. According to Soviet reports, it had been used on two previous orbital flights and recovered undamaged each time.

The cosmonaut was one of a group of pilots who had been preparing for space flight. Their selection and training was in many ways similar to the program for the Mercury astronauts. The Soviet space candidates spent grueling hours in the centrifuge, in heat chambers, in dark soundproof rooms, and in a simulator built to resemble a spaceship's cabin. They too spent a great deal of time studying to prepare themselves for the task ahead.

The man who was chosen to make the first flight, Yuri Gagarin, was a Soviet air force lieutenant who had become interested in aviation at an early age. He was born on March 4, 1934, and spent the years before World War II on a farm with his parents, two sisters, and a brother.

After the war, the family settled in the town of Gzhatsk, where Yuri entered a vocational school to learn to be a molder. His teacher remembers him as a very good pupil, but Yuri was already more interested in aviation than anything else. He took extra courses at a night school and then moved on to a technical school. He also joined an aviation club and learned to fly a Yak trainer. In 1955 he decided to become a military pilot. At the end of a two-year training course, he began his career in the Soviet air force. There he was very busy, but he found time to engage in sports—basketball, skiing, skating, and badminton.

Soon Lieutenant Gagarin heard about the Soviet program for training spacemen. He applied and was accepted as a candidate. And on April 12, 1961, he became the first man to travel in space.

The *Vostok* was launched at 9:07 A.M. Moscow time. Gagarin later reported that the acceleration, noise, and vibration of the launching did not bother him unduly.

Left. *Cosmonaut Yuri Gagarin takes part in a press conference after making the world's first orbital space flight.* Right. *Gherman Titov, the second man to orbit the earth, is helped into his space suit.*

When he went into orbit he found that he quickly became used to the sensation of weightlessness. He was able to do his work, eat, drink water, and observe his surroundings.

The pioneer spaceman was impressed with what he saw. The earth had a beautiful blue halo. The sky shaded gradually from blue to violet, and then to black. The stars were very bright against the black sky. Below him he could make out the larger mountains, rivers, and forests, various coastlines and islands. He could see clouds and the shadows they made on the earth.

The *Vostok* made one orbit of the earth. Gagarin reported that he passed into and out of the earth's shadow very quickly. At the end of the trip, when the *Vostok* reëntered the earth's atmosphere, its outside surface became a ball of fire. The cosmonaut confessed later that he was terrified, but inside the spaceship the temperature remained a comfortable 68 degrees Fahrenheit.

The *Vostok* came down in the Russian countryside, reportedly close to the target area. During the 89.1 minutes it had been in orbit around the earth, its altitude had ranged from 110 to 188 miles. From blast-off to landing the trip had taken one hour and forty-eight minutes at an average speed of 17,000 miles an hour.

What was Cosmonaut Gagarin's opinion of space travel? He is reported to have said: "I would like to do a lot of traveling in space. I like it. I would like to go to Venus, to Mars, to do some real flying."

The next cosmonaut to take a space trip was Gherman Titov. On August 6, 1961, he orbited the earth

17½ times. Like Gagarin, Titov was a member of the Russian Air Force and the two men were friends.

Titov was 26. He had grown up in Siberia, the eastern part of the Soviet Union. His father said that Gherman had been an obedient and industrious boy who liked to make things, especially gliders and model airplanes. He liked to read and he did well at his studies. Titov had always wanted to become a pilot. He entered flying school in 1955. Two years later he passed his pilot's examination with a grade of excellent and entered the Soviet Air Force.

The spaceship used by the second cosmonaut, was called *Vostok* 2. It differed in some respects from *Vostok* 1. Many of its systems had been improved, and it carried equipment to televise continuous pictures of the pilot for the information of scientists back on earth.

Vostok 2, with Gherman Titov aboard, was launched at nine o'clock in the morning. The cosmonaut carried with him the schedule he was to follow during the 25 hours he was aloft. It told him when to send messages, maneuver his spacecraft, eat, and sleep.

When the time came for his first try at taking over the controls of *Vostok* 2, the cosmonaut was worried. Would he be able to steer it? He found to his relief that *Vostok* 2 managed as easily as a car or plane.

After he had made one circuit of the earth and was flying again over the Soviet Union, Titov—or the Eagle, as he called himself while he was in orbit—radioed: "The flight is progressing successfully. All the equipment of the ship is functioning normally. I am feeling well."

During the third orbit it was time for lunch, three

courses which he ate from tubes. Supper came during the sixth orbit. In between, as he had time, Titov radioed greetings to the peoples of the various continents as he passed over them.

The cosmonaut was scheduled to go to sleep shortly after six o'clock Moscow time, after nine hours in space. He sent the following good-night message to Moscow: "Dear Moscovites, there are no changes in the cabin. The pressure is normal, perfect pressure. Humidity is 70 per cent; temperature is 18 degrees centigrade [64.4 degrees Fahrenheit]. I am perfectly comfortable, perfectly comfortable; I wish you the same. Everything is going well, everything is going marvelously. I beg to wish dear Moscovites good night. I am turning in now. You do as you please, but I am turning in."

Cosmonaut Titov slept so well that he woke up 37 minutes late according to his timetable. *Vostok* 2 had been making one trip around the earth every 88.6 minutes during the eight hours that he slept. His journey was nearing its end.

After *Vostok* 2 had traveled around the earth 17 times, the automatic reëntry system went into operation as scheduled. The spaceship left its orbit and began to descend. Like Cosmonaut Gagarin before him, Titov saw the outside of his cabin turn into a ball of fire. Inside, the temperature went no higher than 71.6 degrees Fahrenheit.

As *Vostok* 2 neared the target area, Titov decided to eject himself from the cabin and come down by parachute instead of remaining with the spaceship as Gagarin had done. He landed on one side of some railroad tracks; *Vostok* 2 landed on the other. It was 10:18 A.M., Moscow time; Cosmonaut Titov had been gone 25 hours and 18 minutes. He had covered a distance approximately equal to a trip to the moon and back.

Like their counterparts in the United States, Soviet scientists were interested in finding out how prolonged weightlessness would affect a space traveler. Titov's flight told them some of the things they wanted to know. During most of the time he was in orbit, the cosmonaut was mildly "seasick." He was uncomfortable, but able to continue working. His nausea grew worse up to the time he went to sleep and was especially bad whenever he moved his head quickly. He felt better after he had slept, but he didn't recover completely until *Vostok* 2 began its descent.

On August 11, 1962, Soviet space officials launched *Vostok* 3 and followed it a day later with *Vostok* 4. The two spaceships, each carrying a cosmonaut, were within 3.1 miles of each other during *Vostok* 4's initial orbit of the earth. This "group" flight was followed by another dual launching on June 14 and 16, 1963. *Vostok* 5 and 6, which passed within three miles of one another, brought the *Vostok* program to an end.

Soviet scientists turned next to the development of the *Voskhod* (Sunrise), a spacecraft designed to carry more than one cosmonaut. They also continued to improve their launch vehicles. Only a very powerful and highly developed rocket system could send a manned spaceship beyond an earth orbit, however, so in the Soviet Union, as in the United States, there was still much work to do.

XII. COUNTDOWN

On February 20, 1962, American newspaper headlines proclaimed the story everyone had been waiting for: GLENN ORBITS EARTH THREE TIMES SAFELY. After 1,160 days of hard, painstaking effort, the men of Project Mercury had achieved their goal.

There had been some disheartening setbacks during those 1,160 days, but none were more frustrating than the ones that occurred right at the end. The flight that finally proved to be so successful on February 20 had been postponed no less than ten times!

After the astrochimp Enos completed his two orbits of the earth on November 29, 1961, manned flight around the earth was next on the Project Mercury schedule. Before Enos, an unmanned capsule had made a successful orbit. In both firings the capsule and the Atlas booster had performed well. There was nothing more that could be learned until a man was placed in orbit.

The man chosen to make the all-important trip was— Lieutenant Colonel John H. Glenn, Jr., at 40 the oldest of the seven astronauts. His alternate, the astronaut who would go if Glenn should become ill, was Lieutenant Commander Malcolm Scott Carpenter. The date was tentatively set for some time before the end of the year. It was hoped that, like the Soviet Union, the United States would be able to orbit a man in 1961.

The length of time spent in preparation between the Mercury launchings had averaged about six weeks. After Enos' flight, workers at Cape Canaveral thought that by working extra hours they could be ready in less time. But there was too much to do and too much at stake to take chances on hasty work. The date was finally set for January 16, 1962. And even that proved to be too soon.

During the pre-flight check a defect was found in the capsule's air-conditioning system; it meant a week's delay. The repairs couldn't be completed in a week—another delay. Then there was trouble with the emergency oxygen supply to the capsule's cabin and the astronaut's pressure suit. The date of the launching had to be set back again—to January 27.

This time the preliminary checks indicated that both the Atlas and the capsule were ready to go. Astronaut Glenn, who had been training daily for the flight, was also ready. It looked as if January 27 might be the big day.

The astronaut was up at two in the morning. At 5:15 A.M. he climbed into the space capsule. The moon was shining and everything still looked good for the launching.

Top. *Astronaut John Glenn (left) was selected to make the first American orbital space flight around the earth, with Scott Carpenter (right) as alternate. Bottom. Glenn gets a friendly chuck on the cheek from technician Guenter Wendt after the January 27 flight is postponed.*

At 9:10 A.M. the flight was called off. Several minor
technical difficulties had held up the countdown. While
technicians worked to correct them, an unexpected
cloud cover rolled in over Cape Canaveral. It was thick
and it showed no signs of lifting. Project Mercury officials would not be able to follow the Atlas as it lifted
off the pad. The safety of the astronaut depended on
optical as well as electronic tracking.

"Well, there'll be another day," said the weary
Colonel Glenn as he left the launching pad after four
hours in the capsule.

As it turned out, there were to be several more days.
Fuel had leaked into an insulated bulkhead of the Atlas
missile. The insulation had to be replaced. And then
the weather caused more delays. Like Astronauts Shepard and Grissom before him, Glenn would land in the
Atlantic, and weather is usually bad in the mid-Atlantic
during February. A series of storms moved across the
area. The waiting recovery ships pitched and rolled in
strong winds and waves 20 feet high. A capsule landing
in such seas was apt to be lost.

The storms continued to move in; Cape Canaveral
and the whole country continued to wait. The Atlas
booster and the capsule stood on Pad 14 ready to go.
Astronaut Glenn went over his flight procedures again
and again. Project Mercury was close to achieving its
goal. Everything depended on the weather.

During the frustrating days of waiting there were
some who said Project Mercury was being too cautious;
the officials were too insistent that everything be super-

safe. "All progress involves some risk," they said. "Lindbergh would never have crossed the Atlantic if he had been flying for Project Mercury."

But Mercury officials refused to take any chances. Their job was to send a man into space and into orbit, and then *bring him safely back to earth.* They wanted to learn if man could carry out useful activities while traveling in space. No activity could be called useful if the man didn't come back safely.

There was another reason why Project Mercury was proceeding cautiously. None of its activities were being kept secret. The whole world could watch, and was watching, what happened at Cape Canaveral. The Soviet Union had already sent two men into orbit around the earth. Now it was the turn of the United States. Failure would mean a serious loss of prestige.

The sky was covered with clouds when John Glenn was awakened at 2:20 on the morning of February 20, 1962. Although the weather didn't look encouraging, out at the launch area the final countdown had begun at 11:30 P.M. Breakfast was at 2:45 A.M.—orange juice, scrambled eggs, steak, and toast. The same menu had been prepared for Astronauts Shepard and Grissom, and for Glenn himself, on January 27.

The physical examination, which started at three, lasted an hour. In spite of the weary days of waiting, the astronaut was in excellent shape. And so were the Atlas and the capsule. The countdown was proceeding without a hitch.

At 4:00 A.M. the count was stopped at T minus 120 minutes. This was a planned hold to give the technicians some extra time if they needed it. So far everything was right on schedule. By 4:30 Astronaut Glenn was getting into his 20-pound space suit. Pressure tests to make sure the suit would hold oxygen were next.

At five o'clock he was ready to leave Hangar S for the launching area. It was still cloudy. Astronaut Carpenter and the flight surgeon rode to Pad 14 with Glenn. Pad 14 was a blaze of lights. Shortly after the astronauts arrived, the planned hold was extended for 45 minutes. Trouble had been discovered in the guidance system of the Atlas booster.

At six o'clock Glenn left the van that had brought him from Hangar S. Crewmen working in the launching area could see him smile behind his space visor as he walked briskly to the elevator. There had been some breaks in the clouds, but they had closed in again. Above the capsule, which had been named Friendship 7, the sky was black and forbidding.

The countdown was resumed at 6:26—T minus 120. The astronaut was in the capsule and the hatch was closed, but he couldn't be sealed in. There was a broken bolt on the hatch cover. The bolt had to be replaced. It was now 7:25—T minus 60 and holding. The sky was still covered with clouds.

And so it went with the hands of the clock getting ever closer to nine. There was growing concern about the time. Unless Friendship 7 could be launched before

Top. *Astronaut Glenn, accompanied by flight surgeon William Douglas, leaves Hangar S on the morning of February 20, 1962.*
Bottom. *Mercury-Atlas 6 zooms into the air, launching Glenn on the first United States orbital flight.*

9:30 or 9:45, its orbits would have to be reduced to two or even to one. For a safe recovery there had to be an ample margin of daylight left in the Atlantic landing area.

At 9:30 A.M. the count had reached T minus 15 minutes. Both the astronaut in the capsule and the Mercury officials monitoring the launching were reporting all systems "Go." The clouds that had hung over the Cape were gone. A beautiful sun was shining, and a feeling of optimism had replaced the earlier gloom.

After just one more short delay, the count was resumed for the last time at 9:42. When the clock moved past 9:46, the count was in seconds: nine, eight, seven, six, five, four, three, two, one, zero!

Fire and smoke appeared under the tail of the Atlas. The 130-ton rocket rose slowly from the launching pad trailing a bright, white-yellow flame. With a roar it went streaking skyward followed by a thin white vapor trail. Within seconds it was gone.

From his capsule perched on top of the speeding Atlas, Astronaut Glenn reported: "Lift off, the clock is operating, we're under way."

Friendship 7 was moving toward its orbital altitude. As he rocketed through the area where there was still enough atmosphere to buffet the capsule, the astronaut told the Control Center: "Some vibration area coming up here now."

But he was having no trouble. All his instruments were working and he was reporting their readings to the Control Center in a calm, steady voice. The man

At the Cape Canaveral Control Center, Flight Surgeon William Douglas (left) and astronauts Donald Slayton (center) and Alan Shepard monitor Glenn's historic flight.

who was receiving his messages was Alan Shepard, the astronaut whose ride in the capsule Freedom 7 had made him the United States' first spaceman.

From the moment of launching the men in the Control Center had been greatly concerned with the flight path of the Atlas. Any variation from the planned direction would send the capsule into an orbit over areas where it could not be tracked and where it would be difficult to recover after landing. Likewise, the capsule's speed had to be just right. If it didn't reach a speed close to 17,500 miles an hour at the proper point, it wouldn't go into orbit at all and would have to be brought down at once. Too much speed, on the other hand, would result in an unplanned orbit that might expose the astronaut to dangerous radiation. And when the capsule came down, it might be out of reach of the recovery forces.

The two booster engines of the Atlas had exhausted their fuel two minutes after the launching, leaving the 60,000-pound thrust sustainer engine to lift the capsule into orbit. After five minutes of flight it, too, burned out, and Friendship 7 went into orbit at 17,545 miles an hour.

Computers at the Goddard Space Flight Center at Greenbelt, Maryland, had been electronically monitoring the Atlas since it was one-half of one inch off the launching pad. Within two-and-a-half seconds after the capsule went into orbit, information on its speed, elevation, and direction had been transmitted to Goddard, run through the computers there, and the results sent to the Cape. It was a good orbit!

From the Mercury Control Center Alan Shepard relayed the happy news to Glenn in Friendship 7. "You have a go. At least seven orbits."

That meant that the orbit attained by Friendship 7 was good enough to carry it seven times around the earth. The plan, however, called for it to come down after three trips.

Upon going into orbit, Friendship 7 had turned around so that its blunt end was forward. This enabled Glenn to look back toward Cape Canaveral. Like Gagarin, Titov, Shepard, and Grissom—all of whom had traveled in space before him—the astronaut was greatly impressed with what he saw below him. There was a big cloud pattern stretching all the way to Florida. "Oh, that view is tremendous!" he exclaimed.

XIII. THREE TIMES
AROUND THE EARTH

As Friendship 7 sped across the Atlantic, the Mercury tracking network stood ready to follow its progress with radio and radar. Each one of the 18 stations scattered around the globe was in constant communication with the Goddard Space Flight Center and with the Mercury Control Center at Cape Canaveral. The tracking stations were located so that the astronaut would be within range of one of them for almost his entire journey.

Each time it circled the earth, Friendship 7 would follow a slightly different path due to the earth's rotation. Because the overall orbit pattern had been planned with the possibility of a forced landing in mind, the capsule was routed over the United States and over water as much as possible. Its path swung back and forth across the equator, ranging from about 32 degrees north of it to 32 degrees south.

From the space craft came a constant stream of radioed reports on the condition of the astronaut and his capsule. The station at Bermuda began receiving these reports three minutes after the launching. Then Friendship 7 passed within range of a tracking ship in the

Atlantic and the stations located at Grand Canary off the coast of Africa and at Kano in Nigeria. To the men at Grand Canary Astronaut Glenn radioed: "I am very comfortable. All systems are O.K."

By 10:28 he had eaten two tubes of food, one meat and the other fruit, and some malted-milk tablets. Having left Africa behind him, he was in contact with the tracking ship in the Indian Ocean as he headed toward Australia.

When he crossed the East African coast, Glenn entered the night of February 20. It was still night when he reached Australia. The citizens of Perth and Rockingham, in the western part of that country, had turned on all their lights in the hope that the spaceman would be able to see them. To Astronaut Gordon Cooper, who was the capsule communicator at the tracking station at Muchea, Australia, John Glenn reported that he saw some very bright lights, and he added, "Thank everyone for turning them on, will you?"

Another day dawned as he traveled across the Pacific. Speaking of his first "day" in space, Colonel Glenn said: "That was sure a short day. That was about the shortest day I've ever run into!"

With the coming of daylight, the astronaut saw that his space craft was surrounded by thousands of luminous particles ranging in size from the head of a pin to three-eighths of an inch. They seemed to be moving at the same speed as the capsule. He didn't know what they were, but they caused him no difficulty. At this point he was experiencing no difficulties of any kind.

As he approached the coast of Mexico, however, he

began to have trouble with the capsule's automatic attitude-control system. This was supposed to keep the blunt end of the capsule pointing upward and forward. Instead it was swinging to the right so that the capsule was moving sideways through space. The astronaut reported that he had started to "fly-by-wire," meaning that he was keeping the space craft in a proper position by manual control.

Still flying-by-wire as he passed over Cape Canaveral, but having no trouble controlling the capsule, Astronaut Glenn reported to Alan Shepard in the Control Center on what he thought had gone wrong. From the Control Center came the advice: "Recommend you remain fly-by-wire."

Friendship 7's first orbit of the earth was completed at 11:21 A.M.; it had taken 88 minutes and 29 seconds. Astronaut Glenn was in excellent condition. His electro-cardiogram, respiration rate, and blood pressure were all normal. When asked if he had experienced any of the dizziness and nausea that had bothered Cosmonaut Titov, he had answered: "No symptoms whatsoever. I feel fine."

At 11:26 A.M. the astronaut was again in contact with the Bermuda tracking stations as he started around the earth for a second time. High above the Atlantic the sun was shining brightly. He told the trackers in the Canary Islands: "The sun coming through the window is very, very warm where it hits the suit. I get quite a bit of heat from it."

Top. *From the tracking station at Muchea, Australia, Astronaut Gordon Cooper (in black shirt) and command team follow Glenn's flight.* Bottom. *A picture of the west coast of Mexico taken from an orbiting Mercury spaceship.*

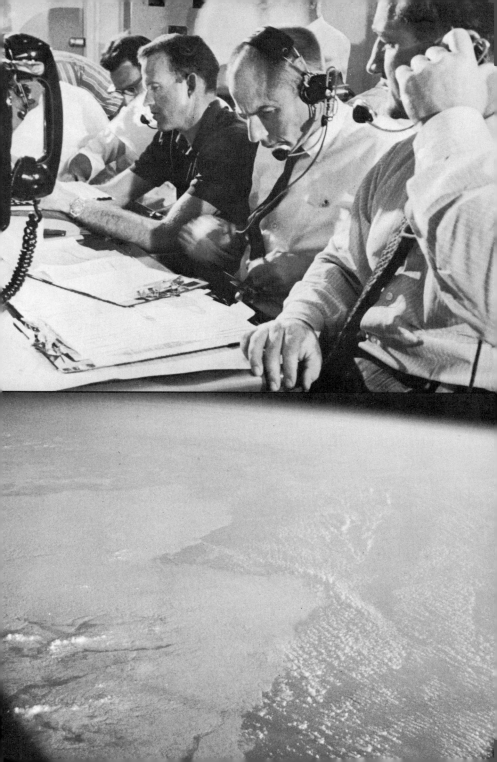

On he flew, across Africa and into his second night over the Eastern Hemisphere. At 12:45 P.M. Glenn was approaching the west coast of the United States for the second time. From Hawaii he had sent word that he was ready to go for another orbit. To Astronaut Wally Schirra at the Point Arguello, California, tracking station, he reported: "I feel real good, Wally. No problems at all."

This was a time of decision for the men at the Mercury Control Center at Cape Canaveral. Should Friendship 7 be brought down because of the trouble with the attitude-control system, or should it be allowed to go on for three orbits? The astronaut seemed to be having no trouble with his manual control of the capsule. The decision was made: Three orbits!

This time, as Friendship 7 flashed over Florida, Glenn worked out some landing details with Alan Shepard at Mercury Control. Crossing the Atlantic for the third time, he got a wide view of the area in which he would be coming down. "It looks very good down that way," he reported. "It looks like we'll have no problems on recovery."

The astronaut's optimistic statement brought little cheer to Mercury Flight Director Christopher Columbus Kraft at the Control Center. Since the end of the first orbit the trackers on the ground had been receiving a signal that indicated the capsule's heat shield was loose. This was a development that caused considerable alarm. Unless the heat shield was in place when Friendship 7 reëntered the atmosphere, there was little

chance that the astronaut would survive the trip back
to earth.

Kraft called in Kenneth Kleinknecht, the newly
named Mercury Project Manager, and Bill Bland, a
Mercury expert. While they were trying to decide what
to do, Astronaut Alan Shepard and Systems Monitor
Don Arabian began going over blueprints and wiring
diagrams to see if they could spot something that could
have gone wrong with the capsule's circuitry. They all
felt that the signal was a false one, but they couldn't
be sure.

The capsule moved on in its third orbit and into
night for the third time in four hours. As it passed
over Hawaii for the last time, a special check was made
on the heat shield. It seemed to be all right; evidently
the signal had been erroneous. After hurried, and worried, consultations the Mercury controllers on the
ground advised Astronaut Glenn not to jettison his retro-rockets after they fired. Their straps would help
hold the heat shield in case it was loose. Spent retro-
rockets had never been retained before. They might
give some trouble on the way down, but not nearly so
much trouble as a loose heat shield.

The astronaut was ready to begin his descent from
space. He had secured all his loose equipment and
checked his control systems. At 2:20, as he approached
the California coast, the retro-rocket firing began—
three braking rockets to slow the capsule and start it on
its downward journey. As they fired against the direction of the space craft, the astronaut received quite a

While Astronaut Glenn was traveling at a speed of 17,500 miles an hour, an automatic motion picture camera installed in the capsule took this picture.

jolt. "I feel like I'm going back to Hawaii," he told Walter Schirra at Point Arguello.

"You don't want to do that. You want to go to the east coast," was the answer.

And that, of course, was exactly the direction in which Glenn was headed, loosing altitude steadily as his speed decreased. Off Florida's east coast the capsule reëntered the earth's atmosphere. The astronaut was in contact with the Cape Canaveral Control Center, and Alan Shepard was giving him landing instructions. Then, as the capsule passed through the ionosphere—the outer regions of the earth's atmosphere—contact was lost for three long minutes. In that area the radio frequencies they were using couldn't get to, or out of, the capsule.

Meanwhile Astronaut Glenn was having what he described later as a "rather spectacular reëntry." The capsule was still carrying the spent retro-rockets. There was a slight bump, and he thought, "There goes the rocket packet." (He had expected the heat of reëntry to burn it off.) Then he saw some "fire balls"—bright, burning chunks of metal—fly past his window. If the rocket packet was already gone, the only thing left to go was the heat shield. If the heat shield was tearing up it meant, as he said later, "a bad day all the way around."

Actually it was the rocket package burning; he hadn't lost the heat shield after all. The heat turned the capsule to a bright orange. With the outside temperature at 3,000 degrees Fahrenheit, Glenn felt like a man inside a glowing fire. When voice communication was reëstablished, his message was: "Boy, that was a real fireball!"

The capsule's small drogue parachute opened on schedule at 21,000 feet, followed by the larger main chute. ". . . the prettiest little old sight you ever saw in your life," said the astronaut.

He splashed into the sea 166 miles east of Grand Turk Island at 2:43 P.M., 4 hours and 56 minutes and 81,000 miles after the launching at Cape Canaveral. His three orbits had taken him from 98.9 to 162.5 miles above the earth.

The astronaut had already been in contact with the destroyer *Noa* of the recovery fleet. Now from the *Noa*, about six miles away, came the message: "Seven, understand your condition is excellent." Then, as the destroyer came closer to the bobbing spacecraft came the further advice: "We expect to pick you up shortly."

Twenty-one minutes after the landing, a slightly scorched Friendship 7 with Glenn inside was hoisted aboard the *Noa*. "My condition is excellent," he assured the waiting world.

The next day, after the astronaut had been taken to Grand Turk Island in the Bahamas for an exhaustive post-flight examination, a team of doctors and technicians confirmed that he was indeed in excellent physical condition. They were unable to detect any ill effects from his 4 hours and 45 minutes of weightless flight or from the 8 g's he had encountered as he returned to earth.

Top. *Glenn stands on the deck of the destroyer Noa.* Bottom. *During the post-flight debriefing aboard the USS Randolph, Glenn enjoys a cup of coffee.*

Astronaut Glenn had been advised to avoid rapid movements of his head and body while he was weightless, but he soon found this precaution unnecessary. In fact he tried out various head movements to see if certain movements or combinations of movements would produce distortion or nausea. The results were negative. He felt no ill effects whatsoever. He was able to manipulate the capsule's switches with ease, and when he ate he swallowed his food without difficulty.

At a news conference Glenn had this advice to offer hungry spacemen of the future: "I think the only restriction probably to food will be that it not be of a particularly crumbly nature like crumbly cookies that have little particles to them that might break off and you wouldn't be able to get these back unless you had a butterfly net of some kind. As long as the food is solid you can hold on to it and get it into your mouth and from that point on there appears to be no problem."

The astronaut was surprised at the speed with which he became used to weightlessness. He had been weightless only 30 or 45 minutes when he was casually parking things in mid-air. He reported this incident: "I was using a hand-held camera. Another system needed attention, so it seemed quite natural to let go of the camera, take care of another chore in the space craft, then reach out, grasp the camera and go back about my business."

A study of the medical data relayed from Friendship 7 during its flight indicated that the astronaut functioned

Congressmen of both Houses listen closely as Astronaut John H. Glenn, Jr., describes his orbital flight.

normally at all times. In fact he had been able to do
more than had been planned for him. The difficulties
with the capsule's attitude-control system had made him
a full-time pilot in space.

In summing up the flight, Project Mercury's operations
director, Walter C. Williams, said: "It was 100 per cent
successful." But Mercury officials made it clear that it
would not have been such a success if Astronaut Glenn
had not been such a skillful space pilot. He had saved
the mission.

There could no longer be any doubt about the wis-
dom and need of sending men into space. The astronaut had used skillful judgment in overcoming the difficulties he encountered. No instrument could do that,
and no instrument could have reported as accurately on
the unexpected, such as the luminous particles that
appeared around the capsule at sunrise.

As a further check on the capabilities of man in space,
Project Mercury sent a second astronaut, Scott Carpenter, on a three-orbit flight on May 24, 1962. Project
Mercury officials felt that the first flight had not fully
tested the capsule or the ground-control system. Also,
they wished to test certain changes made in the capsule
as a result of Glenn's flight.

Carpenter's space ship was named Aurora 7, and his
flight was as successful as Glenn's. It proved to have a
more suspenseful ending, however, for Aurora 7 overshot
the designated landing area by more than 250 miles. For
nearly an hour the watching nation waited impatiently,
wondering if he was still alive. A Navy patrol plane
finally spotted the astronaut floating on a rubber raft near

the capsule. A team of para-rescuemen landed near him with a larger raft, and soon helicopters picked up the men and carried them to the carrier *Intrepid*.

Even before the successful three-orbit flights of John Glenn and Scott Carpenter, NASA officials had planned to conclude Project Mercury with a one-day mission. But first, improvements to the Mercury capsule and changes in flying procedures had to be tested to make sure that such a long flight was possible. Accordingly, on October 3, 1962, Mercury–Atlas 8 was launched from Cape Canaveral with Astronaut Walter Schirra as the pilot. Schirra named his space capsule Sigma 7 and in it he made a highly successful six-orbit flight.

Because both Glenn and Carpenter had used up most of their hydrogen-peroxide fuel supplies before reëntry, Mercury technicians modified the capsule's control system to reduce fuel consumption. In addition, a considerable amount of drifting, or undirected flight, was programmed for MA-8. When Astronaut Schirra splashed down to a safe landing in the Pacific Ocean, he estimated that he had enough fuel left for several more orbits.

Encouraged by the success of MA-8, Project Mercury officials went ahead with their preparations for the one-day flight. They wanted to study the effect of prolonged weightlessness on an astronaut, especially on his ability to function efficiently as a space pilot. They also wanted to test modifications to the capsule that might prove useful in future space programs.

The sixth American to make a space flight, Astronaut Gordon Cooper, left Cape Canaveral's Pad 14 on the morning of May 15, 1963, in a capsule that he had

named Faith 7. During 18 of the scheduled 22 orbits, the astronaut encountered no problems as he conducted various experiments, took pictures, and slept.

While Faith 7 was aloft, weather conditions were ideal throughout most of the world, enabling Astronaut Cooper to see cities and even villages. "It rather surprised me," he reported. "The first time, over the Arabian highlands, going in toward India, I saw individual roads and rivers and Indian villages. I saw also trucks on a road and a train." He couldn't see people, he added, but he did see John Glenn's "fireflies."

During the nineteenth orbit a light on the instrument panel indicated that the capsule was already beginning to feel the pull of the earth's gravity. Hurried tests showed that although the signal was erroneous, certain portions of the automatic system might not work during reëntry to bring Faith 7 out of orbit. Because of this possibility, Mercury officials on the ground advised Cooper to use the back-up manual method of reëntry, which he did successfully even though it had never been used exclusively before.

Faith 7 came down in the Pacific near Midway after 34½ hours of flight. So skillful was Cooper's manual handling of the controls that he landed only 7,000 yards from his recovery ship, the carrier *Kearsarge*.

Although there was still much to be learned about space flight, Gordon Cooper's successful mission, and those of his fellow astronauts, gave us a basic understanding of what man could do in space. Project Mercury had achieved its goal.

One month before his Mercury flight, Gordon Cooper stands beside a recovered space capsule.

XIV. AFTER PROJECT MERCURY

Even before Project Mercury sent the first American astronaut into space, NASA officials began making plans for a bold new venture which they called Project Apollo. They proposed to send a manned expedition to the moon. It was a truly ambitious undertaking, but President John F. Kennedy gave his support to Project Apollo. In 1961 he announced a new space goal for the United States, in the hope of landing Americans on the moon before the end of the decade.

A landing on the moon was much more complicated than anything attempted by Project Mercury. As successful as that program was, it represented just the beginning of the long journey to the moon. To help bridge the gap, NASA organized a new space program called Project Gemini. Gemini means twins and the Gemini space craft would carry two astronauts.

Upon the conclusion of Project Mercury, NASA's seven veteran astronauts transferred to Project Gemini. They were joined by some newly selected men and training began. Meanwhile, the McDonnell Aircraft Corporation produced a larger version of the Mercury capsule for the

Gemini astronauts. The Air Force's Titan II, a more powerful launch vehicle than the Atlas, was chosen as the Gemini booster.

As had been the case with Project Mercury, the first Gemini shots were unmanned ones to test the booster and the space craft. But on March 23, 1965, Gemini 3 carried two astronauts into space. They were Virgil Grissom, who had flown a suborbital Project Mercury mission, and John W. Young, one of the new astronauts. After three orbits of the earth and a safe landing in the Atlantic Ocean, the two astronauts announced that they were pleased with the performance of the Gemini capsule and its Titan II booster. NASA officials were pleased too. Project Gemini was ready to move ahead.

The next Gemini flight, on June 3, 1965, proved to be a big step forward in the United States space program. While Gemini 4 was traveling 120 miles above the surface of the earth, Astronaut Edward H. White II left the space craft and for 23 minutes maneuvered about outside the capsule. His command pilot, Astronaut James A. McDivitt, remained inside. Once the capsule's hatch door had been opened, both men were exposed to the near vacuum of outer space, but their pressure suits protected them. While he was outside the space craft, White remained connected to it by a 25-foot-long combination air hose, communications line, and tether. In his right hand he carried a gun-like maneuvering unit. By pressing two triggers the astronaut could release compressed air through a system of nozzles and propel himself in whatever direction he wished to go.

Although White's extravehicular activity, or EVA, was the highlight of the Gemini 4 mission, the two astronauts carried out several other successful experiments during the four days that they spent circling the earth. And subsequent Gemini flights proved to be equally productive.

Gemini 5 remained in orbit for eight days, approximately the length of time required for astronauts to reach the moon, briefly explore its surface, and return to earth. The two Gemini 5 astronauts, Gordon Cooper and Charles Conrad, Jr., reported no ill effects from their long stay in space. And NASA officials announced: "We've now qualified one of the subsystems for the moon mission—that's the crew."

Because of launching difficulties encountered by Gemini 6, Gemini 7 went into orbit next. It was followed eleven days later by Gemini 6. Then the two pairs of astronauts, Walter M. Schirra, Jr. and Thomas P. Stafford in Gemini 6 and Frank Borman and James A. Lovell, Jr. in Gemini 7, met in space. The success of a journey to the moon would depend in part on the ability of one space craft to locate another when both were many thousands of miles from the earth. By piloting Gemini 6 to within a foot of Gemini 7, Astronaut Schirra proved that two capsules could rendezvous in space. Gemini 6 returned to earth shortly after the successful rendezvous, but Gemini 7 remained in orbit for a record-breaking 330½ hours.

Gemini 8 added still another feat to the space project's list of accomplishments when Astronauts Neil A. Armstrong and David R. Scott docked their orbiting capsule with an orbiting Agena rocket. Docking is the term astro-

A Gemini two-man space craft shown beside a Mercury capsule. The Gemini capsule weighs more than 3 tons— nearly double the weight of the Mercury capsule.

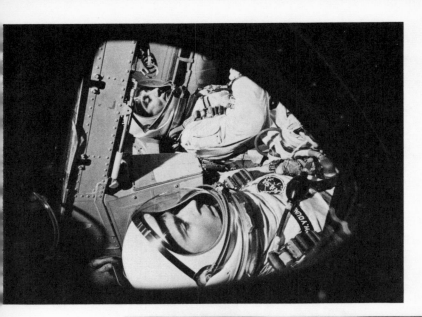

Top. *Astronauts John Young (foreground) and Virgil Grissom wait for the closing of the hatches before the launching of Gemini 1.* Bottom. *Gemini 7 as seen from the hatch
window of Gemini 6 during the first rendezvous in space
of two manned capsules.*

nauts apply to the joining of vehicles in space. When astronauts returned from the moon they would have to dock their lunar landing vehicle with the spaceship waiting to carry them back to earth. Therefore, practice in docking was an important part of the Gemini program.

Gemini's first attempt at docking proved to be quite eventful. A few minutes after the two space craft were joined together, they began to roll and pitch wildly. And when the astronauts disengaged their capsule, the capsule continued to tumble. After some suspense-filled moments, Armstrong and Scott managed to bring Gemini 8 under control, but the mission had to be terminated at the end of the seventh orbit. The trouble was eventually traced to a short circuit that caused one of the capsule's rocket thrusters to fire.

Gemini 9 was a rendezvous and EVA mission flown by Astronauts Thomas Stafford and Eugene A. Cernan. Their landing in the Atlantic near the carrier *Wasp* was recorded by television cameras on the *Wasp*'s deck and transmitted by communications satellite to millions of viewers in the United States and Europe.

Docking was tried again during Gemini 10 along with more extravehicular activity. Astronauts John Young and Michael Collins successfully docked with an Agena target vehicle launched especially for that mission. Then they flew the combined space craft to a rendezvous with the Agena that had been orbiting the earth since Gemini 8's flight.

During the Gemini 11 mission Astronauts Charles Conrad and Richard F. Gordon managed to rendezvous and

Astronaut Edward White walks in space during the Gemini 4 flight.

dock with an Agena rocket in less than one full orbit. The astronauts made most of the complicated guidance calculations themselves, something astronauts on moon flights would also have to do.

The twelfth Gemini flight left Cape Kennedy's Launch Pad 19 on November 11, 1966. During their four days in space Astronauts James Lovell and Edwin E. Aldrin, Jr. docked with an Agena rocket and completed three periods of extravehicular activity.

Their mission brought Project Gemini to a successful conclusion. NASA was now ready to go ahead with Project Apollo. And after the moon, the planets waited to be explored.

Project Mercury had indeed been a trailblazer. The pioneering Mercury astronauts, orbiting the earth in their small space capsule, had tested its systems and observed the effects of space travel on themselves and the capsule. Their flights gave NASA the information it needed for the more complicated missions of Project Gemini. And Project Gemini, in turn, was a preparation for the still more complicated flights of Project Apollo. But neither Gemini nor Apollo would have been possible without the pioneering efforts of Project Mercury. When that program came to a successful conclusion in 1963, the United States had taken a big first step in the manned exploration of space.

Significant Satellites and Space Probes
Before and During Project Mercury

Name   *Launch Date*

Sputnik 1 (USSR)   October 4, 1957
  The first artificial satellite of the earth

Sputnik 2 (USSR)   November 3, 1957
  Carried first living passenger, the dog Laika, into orbit

Explorer 1 (USA)   January 31, 1958
  Discovered inner Van Allen radiation belt

Vanguard 1 (USA)   March 17, 1958
  Contained radio powered by solar cells; obtained valuable
  information on size and shape of earth

Sputnik 3 (USSR)   May 15, 1958
  Carried 2,925 pounds of scientific instruments

Explorer 4 (USA)   July 26, 1958
  Obtained valuable information about radiation levels

Pioneer 1 (USA)   October 11, 1958
  Determined presence of interplanetary magnetic field;
  reached an altitude of 70,700 miles

Project Score (USA)   December 18, 1958
  First radio repeater satellite; carried record of President
  Eisenhower's voice

Lunik 1 (USSR)   January 2, 1959
  First artificial.planet of solar system

Discoverer 1 (USA)   February 28, 1959
  First satellite to go into a polar orbit

Pioneer 4 (USA)   March 3, 1959
  Went into orbit around the sun

Explorer 6 (USA)   August 7, 1959
  Took first crude television pictures of earth

Lunik 2 (USSR)   September 12, 1959
  First probe to hit the moon (September 13, 1959)

Lunik 3 (USSR)   October 4, 1959
  Took first photographs of hidden side of the moon and transmitted them to the earth

Name	*Launch Date*

Pioneer 5 (USA)   March 11, 1960
Went into solar orbit; sent radio signals from more than 22 million miles away

Tiros 1 (USA)   April 1, 1960
First weather satellite; photographed cloud cover

Transit 1B (USA)   April 13, 1960
First navigational satellite; sent radio signals to aid navigation of ships and planes in all weather

Discoverer 14 (USA)   August 18, 1960
First mid-air recovery of orbiting man-made object

Sputnik 8 (USSR)   February 12, 1961
First satellite to launch another vehicle from orbit; first attempt at Venus probe

Vostok 1 (USSR)   April 12, 1961
First manned space craft to go into orbit and return

Explorer 11 (USA)   April 27, 1961
First astronomical observatory satellite

Mercury-Redstone 3
    (USA)   May 5, 1961
First U.S. manned suborbital space flight; Freedom 7

Mercury-Redstone 4
    (USA)   July 21, 1961
Second U.S. manned suborbital space flight; Liberty Bell 7

Vostok 2 (USSR)   August 6, 1961
First manned space craft to orbit earth 17 times

Mercury-Atlas 6 (USA)   February 20, 1962
First U.S. manned space craft to go into orbit; circled earth three times

Orbiting Solar
    Observatory 1 (USA) March 7, 1962
First of new series of observatory space craft; transmitted data on 75 solar flares

Ariel 1 (USA/UK)   April 26, 1962
First international satellite; collected radiation data

Name	*Launch Date*

Mercury–Atlas 7 (USA)   May 24, 1962
 Second U.S. manned space craft to circle earth three times

Telstar 1 (USA)   July 10, 1962
 First real demonstration of the potential of satellites in international communications; carried television, telephone, and telegraph between the U.S. and Europe

Vostok 3 (USSR)   August 11, 1962
 Manned space craft orbited earth a record 64 times

Vostok 4 (USSR)   August 12, 1962
 First attempt at tandem space flight; initial orbit placed Vostok 4 within 3.1 miles of Vostok 3

Mariner 2 (USA)   August 26, 1962
 Closest probe to Venus (within 21,954 miles)

Mercury–Atlas 8 (USA)   October 3, 1962
 First U.S. six-orbit manned space flight

Mercury–Atlas 9 (USA)   May 15, 1963
 First U.S. one-day manned space flight; brought Project Mercury to a successful conclusion

GLOSSARY

Acceleration. The rate of increase in the velocity or speed of a moving object.

Aerodynamics. The study of air as it moves around objects which may be either motionless or in motion themselves.

Afterburner. A device for increasing the thrust of a turbojet engine by injecting and burning fuel in a duct located behind the engine. Sometimes called a *tailpipe burner.*

Atlantic Missile Range. An area in the Atlantic Ocean—extending for 5,000 miles between Cape Canaveral and Ascension Island—over which many U.S. missiles are tested. The range has a series of tracking stations that gather data on the missiles being tested.

Attitude control system. A system that automatically provides control of the position of a rocket or space craft in relation to some reference line or some fixed set of references.

Automatic pilot. A device that automatically steers an airplane or space craft in the desired direction and keeps it at the proper altitude.

Back-up. An item, person, or system kept available to replace one that fails to perform satisfactorily.

Ballistic missile. A missile which is propelled and guided only during the upward part of its flight, after which it follows a path similar to that of an artillery shell as it falls back to earth.

Blockhouse. A structure, usually of reinforced concrete, near the launching pad. It houses the control systems for the launching of a missile, protecting both them and the launching personnel from blast, heat, and possible explosion during a launching.

Booster. A missile's first stage, supplying the initial thrust needed for launching. It usually operates for a very short time. The term is sometimes used to describe the entire rocket system that propels an artificial satellite or space craft into orbit.

Bulkhead. A wall or partition built across an airplane fuselage or space craft to strengthen it or divide it into sections.

Capsule communicator. The man who is in direct radio contact with the astronaut during space flight. The capsule communicator relays information to the astronaut and answers the astronaut's questions.

Centrifuge. A machine which utilizes centrifugal force (the force tending to pull a body away from the center around which it is revolving) to create an approximation of high gravitational forces.

Contour couch. A form-fitting couch made of two layers of fiber glass with foam material between the layers. It is individually fitted to the astronaut to provide him with support during the periods of high acceleration in space flight.

Cosmic rays. Rays consisting of electrically charged particles of high penetrating power. They originate in outer space.

Deceleration. Moving with decreasing speed.

Drogue parachute. A type of parachute used to slow down a space craft as it returns to earth.

Ejection seat. A seat designed to be catapulted or hurled, with its occupant, from an airplane or space craft—usually by an explosive force of some kind.

Fly-by-wire. A system of controlling a space craft in which the astronaut's manual control stick is electronically connected to the jet valves of the automatic system.

Gantry. A frame structure similar to a scaffold used for assembling and servicing large rockets. It allows workmen to reach all parts of the rocket and can be moved back and forth on rails as it is needed.

Geophysics. The physics of the earth and its environment, i.e., the earth, air and, by extension, space.

G-force. Used as a unit of measurement for bodies undergoing acceleration. One g equals the earth's normal gravitational pull. For each g of acceleration a man's body is subjected to a force that is a multiple of his weight. For instance, under a force of 3 g's a 200-pound man will be subjected to a force of 600 pounds.

Gravity. The mutual attraction that masses of matter have for each other. Gravity or gravitation is the force that holds the universe together. *Also.* The attraction of the earth for objects near its surface.

Guidance system. The sensing devices, computers, and other apparatus needed to develop data on the altitude and path of a missile and to translate that data into commands to the missile's automatic control system.

Guided missile. A missile which can be directed throughout its flight either by signals from the ground or by directions originating in the missile itself.

Hard landing. An uncontrolled landing in which the approach velocity is greater than 500 feet per second.

Hydrogen peroxide. A colorless liquid rocket fuel which combines fuel and oxidizer into one substance; also used as a pressurizing agent.

Hypersonic. Capable of moving at a speed five or more times that of sound.

Inverter. A device for changing direct (D-C) current into alternating (A-C) current.

Ionosphere. A section of the earth's atmosphere which extends from about 50 miles above the earth's surface to a height of 250 or more miles. The ionosphere is so named because it is composed of *ions,* or electrified atoms or molecules.

Life support system. The mechanisms in the space capsule that supply the oxygen necessary to keep the astronaut alive, maintain the proper pressure inside the cabin or in the astronaut's suit, remove carbon dioxide and excess water from the capsule's atmosphere, and regulate the temperature of both the astronaut and the cabin.

Liquid fuel. A rocket fuel consisting of chemicals in the liquid state.

Meteor. A body of solid material which originates in space and becomes incandescent with heat when it enters the earth's atmosphere.

Module. A self-contained unit of a launch vehicle or space craft.

Nose cone. The section at the forward end of a rocket or missile which carries scientific instruments, test animals or, in the case of military missiles, explosives.

Orbit. The path taken by a body or space vehicle in its flight around another object.

Override. To use a manually operated control to supplant or neutralize the operation of an automatic control.

Periscope. An optical instrument consisting of a tube, lenses, and mirrors so arranged that a person at one end of the tube sees what is reflected in the mirror at the other end.

Pressure chamber. A chamber within which air pressure, temperature, etc. can be adjusted to simulate conditions at different altitudes. (Sometimes called an altitude chamber.)

Pressurize. To introduce and maintain inside a spaceship, aircraft cabin, or special suit a pressure higher than that which exists on the outside.

Retro-rocket. A rocket fired to produce a thrust against the forward motion of a space craft, thereby decreasing its speed.

Satellite. Any body, man-made or natural, that revolves around a larger body.

Simulator. A training device that reproduces certain conditions of actual flight.

Soft landing. A landing on the moon or other celestial body at a speed slow enough (less than 500 feet per second) to preserve the space vehicle from damage.

Solid fuel. A nonliquid rocket fuel which uses dry chemicals.

Sounding rocket. A research rocket equipped with instruments for obtaining data on the upper atmosphere.

Suborbital flight. Space flight at a speed insufficient to carry the space craft into orbit.

Supersonic. Having a speed greater than sound.

Sustainer engine. The engine that propels a rocket after the engine or engines that supplied the initial thrust have cut off.

Telemetering. A system of recording space or missile data by radioing an instrument reading from a rocket or space vehicle to a recording machine on the ground.

Thrust. The propelling force developed by a rocket engine, usually measured in pounds or tons.

Weightlessness. A condition that exists when the outward pull of centrifugal force equals and therefore cancels out the downward pull of gravity.

Wind tunnel. A tubelike structure into which varying speeds of wind can be blown so that the action of air against airplanes, rockets, or other objects can be studied. Scale models or full-sized objects may be tested in this manner.

INDEX

(References to illustrations are in italics)

LANDMARK BOOKS

WORLD LANDMARK BOOKS